Process Theology

Process Theology
A Basic Introduction

C. Robert Mesle

with a concluding chapter by
John B. Cobb, Jr.

Chalice Press
St. Louis, Missouri

Scripture quotations not otherwise designated are from the *New Revised Standard Version Bible*, copyright 1989, Division of Christian Education of the National Council of the Churches of Christ in the USA and are used by permission.

Quotations marked RSV are taken from the Revised Standard Version of the Bible, copyright 1946, 1952, © 1971, 1973.

Quotations marked JB are excerpts from *The Jerusalem Bible*, copyright © 1966 by Darton, Longman & Todd, Ltd., and Doubleday & Company, Inc. Used by permission of the publisher.

Cover illustration: Ann D. Croghan
Art director: Michael Domínguez

Visit Chalice Press on the World Wide Web at
www.chalicepress.com

10 9 8 7   05

Library of Congress Cataloging–in–Publication Data

Mesle, C. Robert.
    Process theology : a basic introduction / C. Robert Mesle.
    Includes bibliographical references.
    ISBN 0-8272-2945-3
    1. Process theology.   I. Title
  BT83.6.M48 1993   230'.046   93-9204

Printed in the United States of America

Dedication

To my parents, who taught me how to do theology. They taught me, whether they meant to or not, that theology ought to be about values, and that Christian theology, especially, ought to be about love. I have tried to explore the nature of love by asking: "What would a loving God be like?" That's what this book is about.

To Barbara, who believes in this book. And to Sarah and Mark. I love them more than chocolate—even more than our own hot fudge sauce over vanilla ice cream and brownies, with a piece of sacred fudge on the side.

Acknowledgments

Several colleagues have taken their valuable time to offer comments on this manuscript, for which I am very grateful. Roger Yarrington made it all happen, and responded to my course deviations with more patience and kindness than I earned. I am deeply in his debt in many ways. Jim Will continues to be my teacher and friend. Rod Downing changed the course of the manuscript by challenging me with liberation and ecological concerns. Jerome Stone helped without knowing it. Barry Whitney was enormously helpful, especially for a friend I still haven't met. And of course, John Cobb inspired me from the beginning and helped me out in the end.

Irene Shepherd deserves special recognition as one of my earliest advisors on this manuscript. Thanks, Rene.

Howard Booth has always encouraged and supported me, and pushed back against my naturalism in helpful ways. It's nice to be believed in.

My wife, Barbara, deserves special thanks for helping with the chapter on feminism. She has been my teacher now for many years, and will be for years to come.

Many more have helped with suggestions, challenges, and patience over the years. Thanks to them all.

Contents

Part III

Part IV

Introduction

God is love.

1 John 4:16

The ground then for this book is the conviction that a magnificent intellectual content...is implicit in the religious faith most briefly expressed in three words, God is love, which words I sincerely believe are contradicted as truly as they are embodied in the best known of the older theologies.[1]

"**P**rocess theology" is the name for an effort to make sense, in the modern world, of the basic Christian faith that God is love. That is not an easy task. It requires that we rethink the nature of both God and the world.

Why should we need a new theology? Because of evil; modern science; modern studies of scripture and revelation that confront us with their human, historical origins; increased contact with the other world religions; feminism; and our ability to destroy the world through pollution and nuclear weapons. Over the years, I have become convinced that pro-

---

[1]Charles Hartshorne, *Man's Vision of God* (Archon books, 1964), p. ix. Like most process theologians, Hartshorne now avoids sexist language—like *Man* in this title.

1

cess theology confronts each of these realities with answers that make far more sense than most traditional views of God. Although process theologians frequently address environmental, economic, political, and social problems, it seems appropriate for this introduction to focus on the concept of divinity that underlies and motivates such work.

The largest part of this book discusses process theism—a way of rethinking the concept of God as the divine Subject who loves, wills, intends, and acts in nature and human history. We might say that this God is a divine being, but this is likely to cause as much confusion as clarification. Process-relational theists share Paul Tillich's insistence that we must not think of God as one being (however powerful, etc.) among others, whom we might or might not happen to encounter. But process theists do not share Tillich's view that God is Being-itself (or even creativity-itself).

Rather, they conceive of God as a being in the sense that God is the subject of God's own experience, is conscious, loves, intends, and acts. But as will become clearer through the course of this book, God's experience includes the experience of every creature, and every creature's experience necessarily incorporates, in each moment, an experience of God. Thus the vision of how God and the world are interwoven does not neatly fit into either the traditional or Tillichian ways of thinking. It is to remind readers of this fact that I will speak of the process God as the divine Subject. Also, it is important to speak of a process-relational theism as distinguished from the many modern theologies and religious naturalisms that speak of "God" in terms of human love, natural processes, and so forth.

Of course, not all process theists think alike. In the interests of simplicity and brevity, I will simply ignore the technical disagreements between process theologians and focus on the more widely held ideas. The view presented here is my own effort to describe the form of process theism that makes the most sense to me. My goal in Parts I through III is to explain process theism as simply and clearly as I can, so that you the reader may consider for yourself whether it makes sense to you.

Also, I should acknowledge that this book is written primarily for a Christian audience. This is only an expression of my own inadequacy. I don't think I understand other religious communities well enough to have confidence that I can address these thoughts directly to their concerns and perspectives. It should be emphasized, however, that there are Jewish process theists and non-Christian Unitarian process theists, as well as Buddhists and others who are in serious dialogue with process-relational thought. And certainly not all process naturalists would think of themselves as Christians. So if this book should come to the attention of non-Christian readers, I hope they will see that its intent is to address issues that are human, interreligious, and global, and to do so with as great an openness as possible to the values of non-Christian people and religions.

The Meaning of "Traditional" or "Classical" Theology

Throughout this book references will be made to "traditional" or "classical" views of God. Obviously, two thousand years of Christian theology have produced a wide range of understandings of God. Nevertheless, I think it is reasonable to point to a mainstream tradition familiar to most Christians. In the traditional or classical view, God is omnipotent (has all the power there is, can do anything God wants that is not self-contradictory), is omniscient and eternal (stands outside of time so as to see all of time at once, and hence knows the "future" infallibly), and is absolutely unchangeable in every respect. Also, many modern Christians would say that God limits God's own power so as to allow room for human freedom. While I could say more, this should be pretty familiar. So I beg the pardon of those who are keenly aware of the diversity of Christian theology, but hope my approach is seen as reasonable for an introductory book of this type.

The Hard Part: Rethinking Philosophical Foundations

The appeal to common human experience is basic to process thought. The phrase *common human experience* really has two meanings. It partly refers to "ordinary" experiences such as feeling pain, grief, or joy, tasting chocolate, seeing colors, or getting angry. But it also refers to those dimensions of experience that are absolutely universal because they are necessary elements of any experience at all. Process thinkers work hard to derive their beliefs from these experiences. In this respect, many people find that they shared process ideas all along. This makes it easy to explain. At the same time, however, process theology rests on some ideas about the nature of reality that are fundamentally different than those of traditional theologies. If we stayed only at the surface, we could avoid talking about those differences and keep things simple. But that would be bad theology.

It is a simple historical fact that ancient Greek philosophers like Plato and Aristotle have had a profound impact on Christian theology—perhaps as much impact as the Bible has had. But we are rarely aware of the philosophical assumptions about reality that underlie our traditional theologies. People who have never heard of Plato or Aristotle have nevertheless inherited rough forms of their ideas. And it is impossible to make truly fundamental theological revisions without challenging those Greek origins. That will gradually become obvious as you read this book.

When you ask "How does God act?" most traditional theologies have no answer. "He just does!" But process theology is exciting and intellectually responsible precisely because it does try to talk about how God acts in the world. It is by setting the idea of God within a comprehensive view of reality that process theologians are able to address with greater clarity the difficult questions that confront us today. To understand those answers, however, it will gradually be necessary to undertake the challenging task of rethinking our basic views of reality. We must examine the nature of time, power, freedom, and the relationship between minds and bodies.

My strategy is to begin with a very simple overview that is essentially a list of key ideas. Then, still avoiding the most difficult philosophical issues, I want to paint a more connected picture of what I like best about process theology. Only then will we turn our attention to a careful examination of specific issues.

My Motive: Process Theology as an Ethical Model

Is process theology true? Does the God it describes really exist outside our human imaginations? I do not know. Indeed, I think of myself as a process naturalist, and will explore this briefly in Part IV. Why, then, do I defend process theism so passionately in these pages?

First, process theology could be true. It makes sense. It embraces and works with the confusing facts of life, suffering, ambiguity, scientific insight, religious pluralism, feminism, and ecology, while traditional theologies seem to me to view these as embarrassments to be accommodated or explained away. Process theology seems to me to be consistent with itself and consistent with the world I experience. Traditional theologies, in my view, are not. So process theology deserves serious study. It makes sense. It may be true.

Second, however, and just as important, I teach the value of process theology because it has good ethics. Process theology has taught me a better way to think about what the idea of "God" means. Frankly, I find the ethics of the traditional God quite appallingly erratic and often demonic. In the Bible, and in much of Christian thought, God has been described as directly willing and causing great evils: war, slavery, plague, famine, and even the hardness of human hearts. At the very best, God has been depicted as standing by and allowing needless suffering that "He" could easily have prevented. To defend our ideas of God, we are driven to turn our ideas of good and evil inside out to explain why it is really good for God to allow such great suffering.

Process theology has taught me that there is simply no reason to let our old ideas about divine power force us into a corner where we must persuade ourselves that gross evils are really good. It has presented me with a model of a God who is genuinely loving in a straightforward and intelligible sense. The God of process theology does everything within divine power to work for the good.

Many modern theologians would very rightly point out that any vision of divinity or even of nature that humans create must be understood as a model or myth. Process theology, in this sense, is a thoroughly modern "myth" precisely to the extent that it creatively draws upon and leads the way in the very best of our modern struggles to envision the nature of reality, the meaning of love, and the depths of the sacred as we experience it all today.

So even if the God of process theism should turn out not to exist, or even if there is no divine being at all, even if we find it more helpful to think of the entire venture as the creation of myths or models, I am convinced that process theology deserves our most serious attention. The ethical model that process thought shows us can transform our whole way of thinking about religion, life, and values. I urge you to reflect on it with an open mind and open heart.

Because I take the unusual step of including a chapter (Chapter 17) that genuinely challenges the theology presented in this book, it seemed important that process theology have the last word in the strongest way possible. I was delighted when John B. Cobb, Jr., whom I view as the preeminent process theologian, agreed to write a concluding chapter for the book. Specifically, he agreed to reflect on three fundamental questions. Why do we need God to make sense of the world in the process-relational vision? What difference does the process God make in the world of our experience? What other contributions can process thought make beyond those discussed in this book? Dr. Cobb addresses these questions with his usual clarity, insight, and wisdom.

Alfred North Whitehead, upon whose insights much of process thought is founded, offers sound advice for the journey upon which we are about to embark.

> There remains the final reflection, how shallow, puny, and imperfect are efforts to sound the depths in the nature of things. In philosophical discussion, the merest hint of dogmatic certainty as to finality of statement is an exhibition of folly.[2]

Whitehead agreed with Plato that any such effort gives us at best a "likely story." Still, the quest itself deserves and requires passion, just as life deserves and requires conviction and openness alike. Journey with me for a while, even if I exhibit some folly.

---

[2]Alfred North Whitehead, *Process and Reality: As Essay in Cosmology* (The Free Press, corrected edition, Griffin and Sherburne, editors, 1978), p. xiv.

Process Thought:
An Overview

Before embarking on a long journey, it is usually helpful to check a map for a preview of where you are going. The more territory the map covers, the less it tells you about each step along the way. The details of highway exits and back streets, and especially the beauty of the scenery, await later discovery. Still, the large road map is helpful to get us oriented.

This overview is intended to fill that function. It gives you a very condensed survey of the terrain of process thought but without the detailed explanations, arguments, or deeper struggles. As you read through the book, you may wish to return to this overview periodically as these broad statements acquire depth and meaning in your mind. By the end of the book, you should be able to see the larger, beautiful world that this map so briefly sketches for you.

The Process Vision

All things flow. Reality is relational, through and through. Reality is a social process.

Freedom is inherent in the world. To be an individual—whether a human mind or an elementary particle—is to be self-creative. But each individual must create itself out of all that has gone before. Past decisions both provide and limit present possibilities. Within these limits, the future is open.

Experience is rich and complex. The clarity of sense experience is grounded in deeper but vaguer experiences of our relatedness to the world process. Adequacy to this wealth of experience is the ultimate test of our ideas.

The world is rich with life. The universe does not center around human beings, and we are surely not the only creatures to experience pain and pleasure. "Dominion" has proved a tragic theological model for understanding our ethical relationship to this world. Instead, we must come to see ourselves as participants in a complex and fragile web of relationships in which each creature has some value.

Process Theism

God is love. That is, God is the unique Subject, whose love is the foundation of all reality. It is through God's love that all things live and move and have their being. God is the supremely related One, sharing the experience of every creature, and being experienced by every creature.

God's power in the world is necessarily persuasive, not coercive. God acts by self-revelation. God, who is the source of our freedom, *cannot* coerce the world.

Jesus, too, had freedom. He chose to be fully responsive to God's call and love. His life and death thereby revealed the character of God's love and God's call to each of us.

Because God loves perfectly, God suffers with the world, calling us in each moment through divine self-revelation, sharing a vision of the good and the beautiful. God *cannot* overrule our freedom, but awaits our free response, constantly and with infinite patience seeking to create the best that can be gotten from each choice we make.

God is omniscient, knowing everything there is to know, perfectly. But this means knowing the future as open, as a range of possibilities and probabilities, not as fixed or settled.

God is co-eternal with the world and shares the adventure of time with us. There has always been a world of some sort in which God has been creatively active.

God is omnipresent. Every person (indeed, every creature) in every moment is experiencing God as the ground of both order and freedom. God at once makes freedom possible and calls us to choose the good, to choose God's vision for the world. Thus God works in the world by continual and universal self-revelation.

But our experience of God is inherently interwoven with our experience of the world, so that these shape each other. God struggles to reach us through the dark glass that obscures our vision. Thus revelation is omnipresent and ongoing, but always ambiguous.

Similarly, God is the ground of the world's becoming. In nature as in history, God acts in the world by self-revelation. But here, too, the power of God is inherently interwoven with the power of the world.

Every event reflects both the power of God and the power of the world. The world may be more or less responsive to God, but there are no separate events in our world standing outside the laws of nature and history at which we can point and say, "God alone did that."

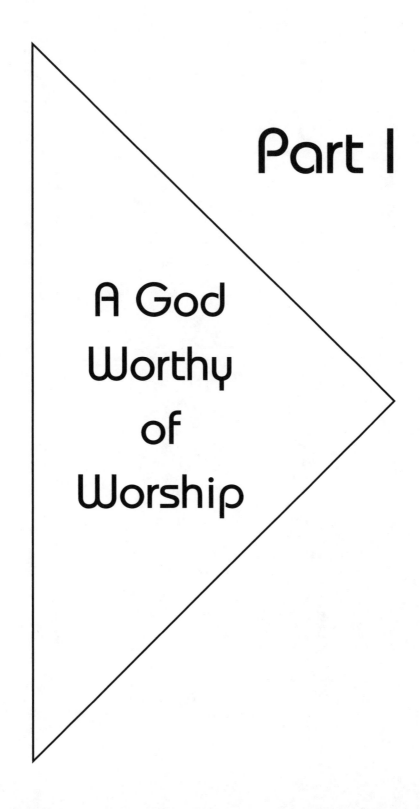

Part I

A God
Worthy
of
Worship

CHAPTER 1

Love, Power, and Worship

It matters if someone loves us. There is no human experience more fundamental to the Christian faith and tradition than the transforming wonder of being loved when we least deserve it. It is the very heart of the New Testament gospel that the life and death of Jesus reveal the unconditional, gracious love of God. "By this the love of God is made manifest among us...," "While we were yet sinners...," "Beloved, if God so loved us..." "We love because he first loved us."

In process theology, God is constantly, in every moment and in every place, doing everything within God's power to bring about the good. Divine power, however, is persuasive rather than coercive. God *cannot* (really *cannot*) force people or the world to obey God's will. Instead, God works by sharing with us a vision of the better way, of the good and the beautiful. God's power lies in patience and love, not in force.

This is not to say that God is "weak" or finite. Process theologians argue that we have simply misunderstood the nature of divine power. A person can lift a small stone. So we think that God, with infinite power, must be able to lift infinitely large stones. A parent can yank a careless child from in front of a car, so God must be able to part the Red Sea and save the Israelites.

But we have hands and God does not. Or rather, when hands are needed, God must rely on the hands of creatures to do that work. Our power is of a kind that arises from our existence in small, organic bodies with eyes, ears, hands, and a nervous system. So while we can lift rocks and yank arms, our power is severely limited in time and space. God has no body like ours (although we might think of the entire universe as God's body). God has no hands of God's own with which to lift and pull. So God cannot do some of the things we can do. God's power is of a kind radically different from ours in most ways—though not without some points of contact. God's power is infinite, everlasting, and universal. God's power is the power that enables all of reality to continue its creative advance, that makes creatures free, that shares the experience of every creature and is experienced by every creature. God's creative power sustains the universe. So God's power is infinitely greater than ours, and very different. Yet, it is only through the creatures of the world that God has hands.

Many people, however, respond initially to process theology by saying that a God who does not have the power to control the world is not really God. Perhaps that is an understandable reaction given our tradition, but I urge you to think past that idea. Is it the power to lift rocks that earns worship? Fundamentally, is it the *power* or the *love* of God that leads you to love God, to worship God, to be willing to commit your life to God's service?

What does it mean for God to be worshipful? Obviously there are many forms of worship. People have worshiped gods out of pure fear, offering sacrifices to appease divine wrath. People have thrown virgins off cliffs, cut the hearts out of slaves, and even murdered their own children out of fear of the gods' anger. (Such gods, of course, are always among us in such forms as war, greed, poverty, and ignorance.) I cannot speak for you, but while sheer wrathful power may force my obedience, it cannot win my loving worship.

Apart from fear, people can also worship in the sense of experiencing awe. This can be more healthy. Certainly most of us stand awestruck before the beauty of the heavens, the majesty of the mountains, and the delicate art of butterflies. Remember, however, that tornadoes are also awesome. Nuclear explosions are awesome. Great evil can be awesome.

For me, the only kind of awe that is authentic worship is the awe inspired by great goodness or value. My reason is simple. To worship properly is to center our lives around something, to see it as the proper focus of our ultimate commitment. Raw power may evoke my fear and even my awe, but not my worship. My worship awaits something, or someone, worth giving my life to.

What kind of God, then, is worthy of worship? If I were to worship any God at all, it would be the ground not merely of existence but of goodness. It would be a God who calls me to be the best I can be, to give the best I can give, to share in a great good work. And a Christian God must surely be one who sets the standard with infinite love.

Process theology is not exclusively Christian. Yet it is no accident that it arose among Christian theologians. On the one hand, you will find in this book many criticisms of the Christian tradition for idolizing power rather than love. At the same time, however, it remains true that Christianity is a religion built around a symbol of sacrificial love—not of coercive power. If Christ is worthy of worship, it is surely not because Jesus could lift large rocks, but because he could touch people's lives, and transform them toward greater love and joy.

It would be a mistake to think that the God of process theology is weak. But process theology attracted me because it forced me to understand that it is goodness, not coercive power, that is worthy of ultimate commitment—of worship. Ethically, God is worthy of love because God is perfectly loving.

Like a friend, but in a way no other friend can, God shares our every experience, our joys and sorrows, our hopes and fears. God is with us in our moments of greatest guilt and despair, yet God's love for us never wavers. In each moment, God takes in our feelings and decisions and responds to them by calling us to redeem from those experiences whatever good can be gotten, and to move from them in directions that can, in the future, yield much greater good.

The difference between traditional views of God's love and power and the process view can be illustrated by two different translations of Romans 8:28. (Please forgive me here for considering this passage without regard for its context. I am not claiming that Paul was a process theologian.)

> We know that all things work together for good to them that love God...(KJV).

> We know that in everything God works for good with those who love him...(RSV).

The familiar KJV translation clearly offers a guarantee about outcomes. All things will work for the good, at least for those who love God. But the RSV rendering is rich in other ideas. God *works* for the good. This is not a guarantee that good will always happen. It is a guarantee about God's character. God works for the good. Where? *In everything*. Process theologians mean this with great seriousness. God works in everything there is to bring about the good. And especially, God works *with* all people (indeed, all creatures) who will respond to the divine call. We could go even further and say that God works with everyone and everything, but the RSV passage at least suggests that God calls for cooperation.

After all, if God were in complete control, what need would God have of our service? It seems obvious that our human religions almost always assume that there is work for us to do, that God is calling us to work *with* God in the world. Certainly Jews and many Christians have understood that building the kingdom is a cooperative effort between God and people.

The battle between good and evil is a real one. God cannot guarantee the outcome within this world. What can be guaranteed is God's steadfast love and constant working for the good. God will be with us in each moment, sharing our struggles, sharing our experiences of sin and suffering, and loving us in the midst of them all.

CHAPTER 2

God's Love
and
Our Suffering

It is commonplace for us all to try to prevent or relieve needless pain and suffering. If a person next to us stumbles and starts to fall we automatically offer a steady hand in support. If someone has a headache we offer aspirin. Parents take their children to be immunized against diseases. We often have no qualms about interfering with the freedom of others in order to prevent needless pain. If a child starts to run in front of a car we will stop her if we can. If we see someone attempting to rape, mug, or rob someone, we will try to stop him, at least by calling the police. If we don't help we will feel guilty.

Everyone knows that painful events *sometimes* work out for the best. Sometimes they can help us grow and mature, teaching us to avoid worse evils and to deal with the suffering that life inevitably will hand us. Given the harsh world in which we live, there is a need for some kinds of learning through pain.

But we also know that not all suffering is needed or valuable. Most of life's suffering produces more harm than good. If a person trips and breaks an arm, or even just skins a knee, he may be more careful in the future, but we still wish we had reached out in time. If someone is raped, abused as a child, or gets cancer, she will no doubt learn something important about life. But no one is glad that these evils exist or wants to experience them for educational reasons. And certainly we do not think that the value of freedom is so great that it justifies allowing rapists, muggers, or murderers to commit their crimes at will. Rape permanently damages the rapist as well as the victim, and both ultimately lose some of their freedom. Indeed, such violent crimes generate fear that assaults the freedom of every member of the society.

Sometimes bad things do become good. I agree that this is true. Indeed, no one affirms more earnestly than process philosophers and theologians that life is complex, interrelated, and ambiguous, and that the meaning and value of events can change dramatically over time. This may be suggested by an informal scale of five responses people might have when looking back from a distance on earlier events that were at the time painful.

1. I'm glad it happened! However painful at the time, that experience taught me a great deal and led me to explore whole new ways of living. The lessons I learned from that event have far outweighed the problems.

2. It was a difficult experience, but I think it was for the best.

3. Well, I've learned a lot from that experience, and I'm a better person in some ways because of it. But if I had a choice, I still wish it hadn't happened.

4. It was a terrible experience. I have learned to live with it and have tried to use it as a learning experience, but it will always be something I deeply regret.

5. It was horrible! Nothing can ever make up for the suffering I endured and still endure.

These are merely suggestive of a continuum of human responses to painful events. Some of these are fairly common, others more rare. An excellent example of number 4, or perhaps even of number 5, is found in Rabbi Kushner's book, *When Bad Things Happen to Good People*. The book arose from Kushner's experience with his son, Aaron, who died the tragic death of rapid aging disease. Part of the power of the book, I think, lies in Kushner's refusal to be glad about what happened to his son. Toward the end of the book he writes,

> I am a more sensitive person, a more effective pastor, a more sympathetic counselor because of Aaron's life and death than I would ever have been without it. And I would give up all of those gains in a second if I could have my son back. If I could choose, I would forego all the spiritual growth and depth which has come my way because of our experience, and be what I was fifteen years ago, an average rabbi, an indifferent counselor, helping some people and unable to help others, and the father of a bright, happy boy. But I cannot choose.[1]

However difficult it is to define evil or badness as philosophical concepts, we all know that bad things happen in this world. We dare not call them good lest we say that the fight against them is misguided.

All of this is common sense. We confirm it by our actions and thoughts many times a day. It is very rare for us to regret that we kept someone from injuring themselves or others, thinking in hindsight that they would have been better off for the pain. It is far more likely that we will feel guilty for having failed to help when we could.

There are, of course, times when we must allow people to take risks. Children learning to ride bicycles must finally be allowed out of their parents' protective reach. But you will certainly understand and approve when I tell you that when our children were learning to ride their bikes I did plenty of running. Whenever possible I kept them from falling. And even now I warn them to be careful. Allowing children to crash into the cement and gravel does not help them to learn

---

[1]Harold Kushner, *When Bad Things Happen to Good People* (Schocken Books, 1981), p. 133f.

how to ride. It only creates pain and fear and slows down the learning process. If I could, I would attach a magical device to our kids' bikes that would make it impossible for them to ride out in front of cars and trucks. But I can't, and neither can God.

Indeed, if you and I could, we would make the world be very different. Did you know that modern medicine has actually eliminated smallpox, a disease that killed millions of people in the past? It's true. And at least in the more developed nations, it is rare for anyone to get diseases like measles, typhoid, typhus, tetanus, malaria, diphtheria, or polio. If you and I could, we would gladly snap our fingers and eliminate cancer, AIDS, MS, and all the other diseases we could think of—even the common cold. Wouldn't we?

The big question, then, is: Why doesn't God do these things?

It is true, of course, that God's values are not exactly the same as mine. I am selfish and self-centered and shortsighted in ways that God would not be. So no thoughtful person confines God to a merely human perspective. All the same, it seems pretty obvious that if words like *good* or *loving* apply to God even remotely like they apply to people, then God must want to prevent broken arms, cancer, and rape as much as we do—indeed, far more because God's love is greater.

Given the appropriate qualifications just mentioned, process theologians assume that God's love is very much like ours, only infinitely greater. God fully shares the pain of the person with the skinned knee. In fact, God even shares the experience of the damaged cells themselves, as well as the more complex and conscious pain of the person. So God hurts with us. God, then, has far more motive than we do to prevent or ease suffering in the world. Allowing for that portion of the world's pain that may finally produce greater good, there is still a whole world full of needless and terrible suffering God would wish to prevent.

Why then doesn't God prevent suffering? Process theology answers that God wants to, but cannot. At least, God cannot do so simply by willing it. Although, as we will see later, there may be some direct role God can play, God's primary role is to draw us to be more active in preventing suffering. God has no hands but ours.

We have not yet discussed just *how* God can act in the world, except to say that God's role is persuasive rather than coercive. Pending clarification (Part II), we can still say something very important about God's love and God's action in the world. *God is constantly doing everything within divine power to prevent and ease needless and destructive suffering.* That, after all, is what we would expect from someone who is perfectly loving.

In a moment I want you to compare that with traditional theism. But first, we must address another problem.

Understanding "Logical Consequences"

People often hold contradictory beliefs. Imagine that someone says they have exactly two apples in one hand and two in the other. You might say, "So you have four apples." Imagine how you would feel if they replied, "I never said I had four apples!" They might say, "I believe I have two apples and two apples, but it is entirely unfair of you to say that I would ever claim to have four apples. I don't believe that at all." You would feel frustrated at their failure to see the obvious implications of their own words.

In the same way many people are frustrated when traditional Christians don't seem to acknowledge the obvious implications of their beliefs about God. We sometimes hear testimonies of how (people believe) God saves one person's life in a plane crash. They then sing praises of the divine power and goodness. But why didn't God save the 104 people who burned? Aren't we forced to say that since God loved them all and could have saved them all, God's allowing 104 people to die in flames was as much an act of divine love as was saving the one? So it must have been *good* from the divine point of view to let the people die or else God would have saved them, too. People rarely say that, but it seems to add up.

Or imagine a rape. If any human being was there and in a position to prevent it we would call it an act of love to prevent the rape. Preventing the rape would be a good thing. Yet, if God is all powerful, God could have prevented it in any of a thousand ways. Perhaps the Holy Spirit could just touch the potential rapist's heart with a small sense of compassion that turns him away from the crime and sets him on a different life path, saving the victim and her family from a lifetime of anguish. Or God might do something more dramatic, rather like the apostle Paul's conversion experience. God apparently chooses not to do this. Why not? Does God love the woman and the rapist? Of course, we say. So God's choice must be motivated by love for them. So if, in God's infinite wisdom, it is loving to allow the rape, it must be (from the divine point of view) a good thing for God just to stand by and allow the woman to be raped. What is loving and even morally required of human beings is the very opposite for God. Again, people rarely say it that way, but doesn't it add up?

If we believe that God is all-powerful we are driven against all our best values and common sense (whether we mean to or not) to argue that rape, famine, plague, child abuse, and cancer ultimately must be *good* in God's eyes or else God would have prevented them. At the very best, we are driven to say that it is good for God to *allow* us to rape, starve, abuse, sicken, enslave, drug, and destroy ourselves and each other in the name of freedom. We are forced by the old idea of God's power to say that what is morally *right* for *us* (protecting the innocent, healing the sick) is morally *wrong* for *God* to do (except one time in ten million when God graciously performs a miracle). Or, traditional views of God force us to say that *what is loving for God* (to allow torture, disease, war, and natural disasters that God could prevent) *is unloving of us*. I cannot tell you how strongly I reject that whole way of thinking, and I believe they are all logical implications of traditional theology—whether people ever say them or not.

Can you imagine that Jesus would have just stood by and done nothing while a woman was raped? I think that Jesus would have done everything within his power to help the victim. (No doubt he also would have been concerned to help the potential rapist, to cause him to "go his way and sin no more.") If you think that Jesus would have helped, and that Jesus revealed divine love, then surely you can see why it doesn't make much sense to say that God *could* stop it but stands by and does nothing because it is somehow the loving thing to do. If it isn't loving for you or me, or for Jesus, why would it be loving for God?

One common answer is that God limits Godself in order to preserve human agency. That is, God *could* prevent evil but *allows* it as a necessary part of human salvation. Morally, I believe this answer just doesn't do the job. It might cover a few cases, but not very many. Allowing evil we could prevent is almost as sinful as directly causing it, as our laws and consciences tell us. There is such a thing as criminal neglect. If a parent allowed a child to burn herself horribly or drink poison or get hit by a car, saying, "It's the best way to learn," we would be appalled. I find it equally appalling that people should attribute such behavior and values to God.

Young children are inclined to believe that their parents can do anything. It is painful for them to learn otherwise. But as a parent, I used to dread the thought that my children might think I *allowed* them to get hurt or sick when I actually was doing all I could to prevent it. Might not God feel the same way? Might not God be deeply hurt by our constant proclamations that terrible evils are "God's will" or are "allowed by God for a greater good"? Surely, if, as process theologians believe, God is doing everything God can to prevent suffering, and if God shares our suffering with us, it must add insult to injury for us to constantly "defend" God by preaching that God really allows such horror out of God's vast wisdom and love.

It is probably a good thing that most of us don't really act on our theologies all that much. Can you imagine someone deciding to follow God's example (in the traditional view) by assuming that whatever God allows must ultimately work for the best? They would never try to prevent pain, error, or even sin. They would assume that skinned knees and concentration camps all work for the best. They would see nothing at all as ultimately evil. Any person who actually *acted* on that belief would surely be locked up as criminally insane.

Fortunately, most of us do not let the traditional "solutions" to the problem of evil direct our ethics. If we did we would think that if God sees it as wise and loving to allow children to be crushed by trucks, then we should, too. But after all, our theologies do have *some* impact on our lives. My very grave concern is just this. To whatever extent people actually let the old solutions to the problem of evil affect their lives, those ideas undermine their resolve to make the world a better place.

Glaring examples of this can be found regarding the nuclear arms race. Some fundamentalist preachers have publically declared that nuclear war will bring about the coming of the kingdom of God and the return of Jesus. If that is so, if nuclear war is really a good thing, why don't we rush out and push the button?

Such a theology, in my view, suffers from the sickness of despair. Confronted by actual and potential evils beyond our emotional and intellectual grasp, we defend ourselves by saying that God has them in hand and either causes or allows them for some good reason. Heaven help us if the leader of a nation with nuclear weapons ever acts on such theology.

Process theology preserves our obvious commonsense values. It acknowledges the crucial distinction between good and evil (however blurry that may be at times) and affirms that God works with all of God's resources for the good and against evil. Our love, at its best, really is like, or at least analogous to, God's love.

We should not behave like the God of classical theology. We should not stand by while people suffer evils we could prevent. But we *should* act like the God of process theology, doing what lies within our power to prevent evil and ease suffering. And when we cannot prevent suffering, we should, so far as our human weakness allows, share it sensitively.

CHAPTER 3

Love, Power, and Relatedness

Process theologians insist that reality is relational, through and through.

Think of someone you love very much. How would you feel if she broke an arm? Won an important award? Broke a promise? Saved someone's life? If you loved her even more, would you share her feelings more or less fully? Think of someone who loves you very much. Has he shared your feelings of joy, sorrow, grief, and triumph? Has he expressed his ongoing, steadfast love in different ways, responsive to changes in you?

In our common human experience it is inescapably clear that love means being related to and affected by those we love. Process theologians believe that these experiences are important guides to understanding divine love. God loves perfectly.

So God must be the *supremely related* One, who shares *fully* the experience of *every* creature, who is at once fully steadfast and fully responsive.

Oddly enough, this obvious feature of God's love has long been denied. One of the earliest ideas to be formally declared a heresy by Christians was "Patripassianism," the belief that "the Father suffers." Given that Christianity is founded on the life of one who "bore our griefs and carried our sorrows," who "suffered and died" on the cross, and whom Christians have declared to be the fullest revelation of God to us, it seems incredible that Christian theologians should deny, for nearly twenty centuries, the belief that God suffers. What made them do it?

Christian theologians denied that God suffers largely because of their understanding of God's power. They believed that God's perfect power put God completely outside of any relationship with the world that might affect God in any way. Understanding why they believed this is crucial to understanding almost every problem this book will address.

Unilateral Power

Think of ordinary examples of power. First, think of kids in a tough neighborhood. The toughest (most powerful) kid can beat up all the others and is beaten up by none. The weakest kids are beaten up by all the others and beat up on none. In between is a hierarchy descending from the most to least powerful. Because this same kind of social structure is seen in chickens, it is often called a "pecking order."

Try sports. The most powerful football team scores easily and is rarely scored upon. Try money. The few richest people have the most power. They can tell other people what to do, but the others cannot tell the richer people what to do. The poorest people, of whom there are millions, can't tell anyone what to do and are at the mercy of those who are richer. Armies provide the clearest examples. Generals give orders to majors, majors to sergeants, and sergeants to privates, but not the reverse. Such institutional hierarchies are designed for efficiency rather than creativity, but they rarely provide either one.

In short, our ordinary approach to power is this: *Power is the ability to affect others without being affected by them.* We can call this *unilateral power* because it runs only one direction, from the top of the hierarchy down to the bottom. Furthermore, power and social value go together. The more powerful you are the more you are treated as a valued member of the gang, the team, the company, the society, or the army.

Just as important, our ideas of power fit our ideas of reality. Often the more powerful something is—especially the more power it has to resist being affected by anything—the more real it seems to us. Shadows and clouds seem less real to us than iron bars and mountains. The power to resist change enables things to endure, and the power to endure makes things seem more real.

There is a direct connection, it seems to me, between these views of power, value, and reality and our fear of pain and death. People who are tortured are totally at the mercy of others. Victims are at the bottom of the hierarchy. Pain and death are the ultimate human cases of being affected and changed. We cling to what we hope will save us from pain and death—from being affected. We admire, envy, and want to unite with those who seem to have such power.

Think of the "macho" man who is strong, in control, impervious to pain. We have traditionally valued such male models, turning to them for protection and security. It instantly becomes obvious why "real men" don't cry. To cry is to admit that one is affected, vulnerable, related. In the traditional way of thinking, to be related, vulnerable, affected, emotional, sensitive, caring, nurturing—in a word, feminine!—is to be weak, not valued, even somewhat unreal. No wonder Hebrews and Christians have thought of God as Father.

In Western philosophy, this whole set of ideas has been reflected in the idea of a "substance." Substances, in that view, are the most real things. A substance is that which endures unchanged through change. It is that which exists independently, needing nothing but itself in order to exist. (Doesn't that sound like financial security? Doesn't it sound like someone who never has to be afraid? Don't you want to be like that?) Two prime cases of substance are God and the (divinely created) human soul.

Strictly speaking, of course, God was declared the only true substance. Only God has perfect unilateral power. God has absolute power to control everything. God also has absolute power to resist being affected by anything. Indeed, God is *almighty*, having *all* the power there is. This is central to the traditional or classical view—the notion of divine omnipotence as perfect *unilateral* power.

The concept of unilateral power can certainly be found in the Bible, but it was the Greek philosophers who honed the idea of perfection. Although their ideas about divinity were very different from ours in most ways, they still laid down fundamental ideas that later Christian theologians accepted. They were good systematic thinkers, and carried through with honest consistency this idea of perfect unilateral power. If God has perfect unilateral power, then God is utterly unaffected by the world—perfectly unchangeable. Nothing at all can change the divine in any way.

The Greek philosophical models were art and math. A beautiful statue can affect the viewer. It can fill us with the desire to be braver, more merciful, more noble in spirit. It affects us. Yet the statue does this without being affected by us at all. It does not pity us, love us, or get angry with us. The same is true in a different way with math. They saw triangleness, squareness, and 2+2=4 as eternal, perfectly unchangeable truths that order the world. We cannot violate their order, yet they do not "give orders." They do not weep or laugh or shout. They are utterly beyond being affected by the world. They are beyond passions, beyond changes of knowledge, changes of mood, or changes of intention. They never act. They are beyond love.

The Greek philosophers understood all of this, and their ideas about God reflected it. They saw that "God" could order the world both in structure and morals without ever being affected by it. So they envisioned the ultimate reality as eternal, unchangeable, passionless.

Yahweh, the God of the Bible, was described as very powerful, too. And in many respects Yahweh's power was unilateral. But Yahweh was also very changeable, filled with passions like anger, jealousy, wrath, sorrow, and even repentance. Yahweh was often depicted as changing his mind in response to the pleadings of Abraham, Moses, and others. Especially, Yahweh was filled with love, was deeply affected by his creation, was in constant relationship with the world. Yahweh was often pictured as being cruel, even erratic, but almost always as involved, related, and caring about creation.

Jewish Christianity began with Yahweh as its model of God. But Christianity very soon became a religion of Gentiles. The New Testament texts were all written in Greek! Gentile Christians naturally began to think of God in the Greek categories familiar to them. It is for this reason that they felt forced to deny, to declare as heresy, the idea that "the Father suffers." To suffer, they believed, is to fall prey to the worst of those mortal weaknesses that God must be above. For nearly two thousand years Christian theologians have been trying to merge the Greek and biblical ideas of God. I believe they have never succeeded.

If God cannot suffer, cannot be affected in any way, then God cannot love. To love is to be affected. But perfect unilateral power is the power *not* to be affected. To love is to enter into intimate relation with others. But perfect unilateral power is the power to be independent—*not* related. To love is to feel all the passions of joy, sorrow, grief, fear, hope, and triumph that bind us to each other, that make life so dynamic and changeable. But perfect unilateral power is the power to be *unaffected* by such changing passions. A God with perfect unilateral power cannot love in the sense in which we love.

Christians always have affirmed God's love—but in what sense? Partly, of course, ordinary people rarely think about it and have a more naively biblical view of God. They pray to God expecting God to respond, to act, to feel. But even ordinary people no doubt appeal to the absolute eternity and unchangeability of God when they want to assure themselves of their own immortality, or explain why God fails to act on their behalf.

More systematic theologians finally arrived at the conclusion that God loves us without passions. God is rather like the statue. We may feel that it is looking at us in a loving way, but it does not feel love. More strongly, God may, out of sheer overflowing goodness, do good things for us, but not because God *feels* sorrow or pity or compassion.[1]

Perhaps the details of these arguments seem puzzling. Perhaps you wonder why anyone would think that way. But it is true that the idea of perfect unilateral power led directly to

---

[1] For an excellent discussion of this, see chapter 3 of *Process Theology: An Introductory Exposition* by John B. Cobb, Jr., and David Ray Griffin (Westminster/John Knox Press, 1976).

the conclusion that God cannot suffer, cannot feel for the world, cannot love in the human sense of entering into genuine, *mutual relationships* with the world.

Relational Power

Process theology operates on an entirely different model of power, reality, and value. Relatedness is primary.

In process thought, relational power is the ability *both* to affect *and* to be affected. But being affected does not mean being passively controlled by others. Relational power involves three stages.

First, relational power is the ability, the *power*, to be open, to be sensitive, to be in relationship with the world about us. Obvious examples are those whose intelligence enables them quickly to grasp complex ideas and events around them; artists who see the richness of colors and hear subtle combinations of sounds; poets who revel in the wealth of words spoken; parents who are sensitive to the feelings, struggles, fears, and hopes of their children.

Second, relational power is the ability to be self-creative. It is the capacity to take in a wide range of ideas, feelings, influences, and experiences and create one's own thoughts and feelings and decisions out of them. Self-creativity is the ability to integrate the world into a unified self, rich in relationships but unique in response.

Finally, relational power is the ability to influence others by having first been influenced by them. It is the power of loving parents to act toward their children in a way that takes sensitive account of the needs and desires of their children, while yet looking beyond the childish perspective. It is the ability of the good teacher to understand the questions and insights and limitations of the students so as to help them learn in appropriate and creative steps.

Gandhi is a wonderful example of relational power. Rather than sit in a tent with the wealthy and "powerful" few, he went to live with the many, to share their work and eat their food, to understand by participation with them their fears, hungers, and dreams. Yet, he had a vision larger than theirs, a sensitivity to the British that was more compassionate than theirs. Especially, he had the capacity to suffer, to be affected by all of those about him, without losing himself. He did not unilaterally shut the others out. Instead, he relationally took them all into himself and created a vision that took account of them all. It is for this reason that the people chose to follow him. He led them by creating a dream in them that reflected their own hopes but called them to larger vision.

Obviously, Jesus also lived out relational power. Paul's insight was crucial—that it was the *crucified* Christ, the Christ who redeemed through suffering, who revealed both the wisdom and *power* of God (1 Corinthians 1:18–24). Regretfully, I think, Christians have thought that this power was not enough. Many have suggested that Jesus could have called down twelve legions of angels if he had wanted to. But twelve legions of angels exercising unilateral power, however great, could not have made a single soul more loving, could not have redeemed the woman taken in adultery, could not have produced the fruits of the spirit that are "love, joy, peace, patience, kindness, generosity, faithfulness, gentleness, and self-control" (Galatians 5:22b–23a). We would never have said of twelve legions of angels wielding swords, "by their wounds we are healed."

Summary

It is important to make a distinction between two different meanings of the claim that God is unchangeable. Process theologians certainly affirm the Christian tradition that declares that God *is* love, that God could never stop loving, or love us less on one day than another. In biblical language, God's love is steadfast, sure, trustworthy. In this sense, God's love is certainly unchangeable.

In another sense, however, it would make sense to say that God's love is perfectly changeable. That is, God's love is fully responsive to the world. In each moment, God shares the experience of every creature and responds to that creature in a way appropriate to it. So while it is probably more helpful to say that God's love is *responsive*, we should recognize that we depart from much of the Christian theological tradition when we affirm this. Traditionally, it has long been denied that God could be genuinely responsive, because responsiveness is a kind of change, and it was held that God could not change in *any* respect.

Probably you have always believed that God was affected by the world, that God was responsive and active and in relationship with us, sharing our experiences and reacting to them. Probably, with regard to God's love, you were a process theologian all along.

In Part II, I will explain in what way process theologians believe that God's love is the foundation of all reality.

CHAPTER 4

Freedom, Time, and God's Power

Does God experience time? If so, how? Strictly speaking, most theologians have said that God experiences no passing of time. God exists in a timeless eternity. In different words, all of time is spread out before God like a picture, so there is no difference between past, present, and future. Where did this idea come from and what does it mean for human freedom?

Aristotle, a Greek philosopher, shared the idea that God has perfect unilateral power, and so described God as the "Unmoved Mover." God caused the world to move and change, but God was totally unaffected—unmoved—by the world. Aristotle also saw a very important implication of this view of divine unchangeability. He held that God had no knowledge of the world.

Knowledge, experience, and activity are fundamental features of anyone's identity. Aristotle recognized that the world is constantly changing. If God has knowledge of the world, then God must constantly be having new experiences and new knowledge. Indeed, every moment will bring a whole world of new information—new experiences—to God's awareness. And if we allowed this world of new experiences to be flooding into God's life in each moment, we might also feel compelled to imagine God as actively responding to that knowledge.

Remember that in the Greek idea of perfect unilateral power, God was absolutely unaffected by anything. Obviously, they thought, God could not be engaged in any such dynamic relationship as knowledge of a changing world would necessarily involve. Aristotle held, then, that God had no knowledge of the world.

Christian theologians could not follow Aristotle's path, but they recognized his problem. The solution they chose was essentially to deny that the world changes. (Our experience of change would then be a kind of illusion.) That would allow God to have knowledge of the world without having knowledge of change and so without being changed.

Think again of that traditional image of time with which we began—as a vast picture spread out before God. God sees all of time as fully present, fully actual, fully settled. The picture, like a tapestry, might tell a story with a beginning and end. But the end of the story is already there, painted in complete detail, never to be altered.

A more modern image might be a phonograph record. Imagine the blank piece of black vinyl set into a press. The master disk is pressed down on the blank and—pssst!—the grooves are stamped onto the record. All of the "music" is stamped out at one instant, the last bar at the same moment as the first. In some respects, that is a good image for how Christians have said God created time—all at once, in a single instant.

When the record is put on to play and the needle set in the groove, music comes out in sequence. If we think of ourselves on the tip of the needle, we can see why it seems to us that time moves from beginning to end. There is a sense in which it does move for us. Notes suddenly leap out and then fade to be replaced by others. Time seems to us to pass, but from God's point of view, it does not.

As both of these images suggest, the classical tradition has been able to grant God total knowledge of the world of "time" while yet protecting God from any change, because ultimately the world does not change. To be fully consistent, we must also deny that there was any time before God decided to create time, or before God did create it, or between God's decision and action. These, too, are part of God's timeless eternity. God has eternally decided to create, and has eternally created. So we can see that in the classical view all of time has actually existed for God in a timeless, absolutely unchanging eternity. Only in this way can we retain God's perfect unilateral power to remain totally unaffected by the world.

It should be obvious now why so many Christian theologians have held a doctrine of total predestination. Although this is not the only reason why this doctrine has been affirmed, it is sufficient by itself to have driven consistent and honest theologians to that conclusion. The end of the story is just as finished, just as actual, just as present to God as is the beginning. Nothing can change. Nothing can be different than God created it as being from all eternity. God knows eternally with absolute and unchanging infallibility what you are doing in this piece of the picture right now. It is all "now" to God.

Martin Luther may have been among the most honest of Christian theologians in holding that given the classical Christian view of God human beings must have no freedom. But many Christians have not understood this or have been reluctant to admit it. They have wanted to claim that we still have freedom. How have they done this?

Often we think of freedom as simply doing what we want to do. That is the sense in which Christian theologians have been able to affirm that we have freedom despite God's perfect foreknowledge. Suppose God predestined us both to sin and to have wanted to sin. We might then claim that we sinned "freely" (we did what we wanted to do) even though we could not have done otherwise, because God predestined us "both to will and to do" the sin.

Obviously, however, this is not the sense in which we usually speak of freedom. In the important moral sense, freedom is the ability to choose between two or more options, as to sin or not to sin. Unless an option is a real possibility, is really open to us, we would say we are not free to choose it. If the traditional Christian views of God's power and of time are correct, there is no such thing as freedom of choice. We could never do anything other than what God has predestined us to do.

There is another way in which some Christians have tried to reconcile God's perfect foreknowledge with human freedom. They say that God can know something without causing it. Often, it is observed, we know what people around us will do just by knowing them well. People are predictable, and the rest of the world is even more predictable. So why can't God, who knows us perfectly, be able to foresee perfectly what we will freely choose to do?

If we set this in the context of the whole view of God's power and the traditional understanding of God's relationship to time, including the affirmation that God is the sole creator of the world of time, then it is obvious that this whole line of thought is irrelevant. In the classical tradition there is no difference between what God wills and what God knows and what God causes. It is all the same.

Nevertheless, let us consider the idea that God foreknows without causing our choices. It is obviously true, after all, that we often know what will happen without causing it ourselves. So let us imagine God for a moment as purely an observer of the world, having no causal power at all. Couldn't God have infallible knowledge of the future, even of our free choices?

No, not if we are truly free. Think again about our ability to predict the future. We have some power to predict because the world is partly determined. Laws of nature limit our options. There is much that we are not free do to. God could certainly have perfect knowledge of those limits. Further, the past—our genetic heritage, our education, our own choices, all our experiences—strongly inclines us to act in certain ways. The past shapes the future. The fact that we can predict the future at all depends on all these limitations on our freedom. If the past *totally* determines the future, if heredity and environment, for example, combine to completely control our actions, then there is no true freedom and God can perfectly predict the future.

But the whole idea of freedom is that the past does *not* totally control the future, but only shapes it. Given my past, there may be a 75 percent chance that I will choose to eat the sausage and eggs I have planned for tonight's supper. There is a 15 percent chance that I might join my in-laws for supper, a

5 percent chance that I may skip supper to make up for eating too many snacks while I write this afternoon, and several other possibilities I cannot even think of right now. What freedom means is that I really do have genuine choices in front of me and that I really could do different things, even though some are more likely than others.

If this description of reality is correct, then if God has perfect knowledge of the world and of me, God will know exactly what all of the possibilities are and how probable they are. But even with perfect knowledge God could not know what I will choose in the future because that choice has not yet been made and it is a real choice. For God to predict perfectly, based on perfect knowledge of the past, the past must totally determine the future "choices." That is, they wouldn't be real choices at all.

Think of it this way. Suppose I am trying to decide whether to have sausage or soup for supper. If we say that God knows I will choose sausage, and that it is impossible for God to be wrong, then aren't we saying that it is impossible for me to choose the soup? We don't have to say that God caused anything. But there must be some way in which God has that knowledge. It may be that the world is a deterministic world in which the past totally controls the future. It may be, as Christians have traditionally said, that all of time is eternally present to God—that my "choosing" the sausage is an eternally settled fact. But whatever the reason, perfect divine foreknowledge means that real freedom is impossible.

Process theologians believe in freedom. They believe that while the past does have a powerful impact on the present and future, there remains room for genuine freedom. Also, as we have seen, they reject the whole approach to unilateral power that originally drove Christian theologians to deny the passage of time. So in process theology, divine omniscience—God's perfect knowledge—means that *God knows everthing there is to know.* But the future does not exist yet, except as a range of possibilities that have not yet been chosen.

In process theology, time is not like the grooves stamped onto a record. Instead, time *becomes,* like music improvised by a jazz combo. The musicians have some idea where they are going, and the choices they have made so far suggest directions for the future. But the whole point of improvisation is that they are making up the music as they go. They can change keys, change tempo, suddenly shoot off in response to a new idea. After playing seven notes of a scale they may choose *not* to play that eighth note, but leave a silence and start off in some totally new direction.

Following the image of the world as a jazz combo, we might play with the idea of God as the lead flute player. God has power to shape the music by God's own choices of what notes to sound. To the extent that the other players are sensitive and *choose* to follow God's lead the revelation of God's musical vision has power to shape the becoming of time. But the insensitivity of the world and the world's choice to create its own music mean that the music is not always what God would choose.

Freedom and Grace

The Christian struggle with freedom is also deeply tied to the historical debate over grace and works.

At its very best, the concept of grace is rooted in the human experience that people must be loved if we are to become loving. Long before we *do* anything to merit love, we depend on the love of parents and friends to touch our lives. As we grow older, we discover that there are moments in our lives when it seems beyond our power to care for others. We may be so filled with pain, anger, fear, insecurity, or hate that we only want to strike out at others. If we are lucky, we find people who love us so much that they are willing to bear the burden of our selfishness, and love us anyway. The more we learn about ourselves, the more we learn that the quality and quantity of love we are able to give surely reflect the quality and quantity of love we receive. The love of others empowers us to love. This is the essence of grace. And in Christian experience, God is the supremely loving other.

Too often, however, Christians have found themselves setting grace and works against each other, so that more grace means less human responsibility. Consider the view of total divine predestination. In this case God is fully in control—exercising perfect unilateral power—and we can claim no credit for our salvation. We thus avoid any grounds for human boasting, and God deserves total credit for any good we receive. Pure grace. Now suppose that some small step in our road to salvation depends on us—perhaps our free decision to believe in Christ. If this step really depends upon us—is a truly human "work"—then we seem forced to say that God is not fully in control, and that we can pat ourselves on the back for "meriting" at least some of the credit for our own salvation. Suddenly, human pride rears its ugly head and the divine victory over evil is no longer assured! So Christian theology beats a hasty retreat back to pure grace. In such a framework, grace and works seem opposed to each other: more works means less grace; more grace means less works.

Some causes for this narrow vision of grace relate to the concept of unilateral power we have discussed. Where doctrines of total predestination have triumphed, *grace* has meant that God alone determines our fate. If God's judgment upon us could be contingent upon our free decisions then God seemed weak, out of control. If God *needed* or benefited from our love, then God seemed incomplete, dependent, and perhaps even selfish—buying our love with gracious admission into heaven. By totally divesting human beings from any role in their own salvation, it seemed to many that God could be praised more highly for being all-powerful and utterly unselfish (gracious) in love.

If, however, we conceive of salvation as quality of life, then it seems obvious that grace and works go together. If, as Paul says, "God's love has been poured into our hearts through the Holy Spirit that has been given to us" (Romans 5:5b), then the natural response is for that love to spill out of our lives into the lives of others. Being filled with love, we become more loving. And as we *choose* to love, we open ourselves further to let that love pour into our hearts, further empowering us to become still more loving. While divine grace always comes first, before human decision, they ultimately work together.

In process theology, divine power *creates* creaturely freedom rather than destroying it. It isn't "grace vs. works" but "works because of grace." Process theology embraces the confession of 1 John 4:19: "We love because [God] first loved us." Indeed, in process theology, every creature in the universe is continually experiencing the divine love. This love is the very foundation of freedom and of love within all creatures. This gracious—unmerited—love is continually poured into all creation. The choice lies with us how we will respond. We have the power to accept or reject that love and the call it involves. But this power to choose is itself a gift of grace.

I do not wish to make the issue seem oversimple. But I do believe that process theism brings excellent values and resources to this discussion. The core of it is this. More grace means more freedom, not less. And the more we freely respond to God's gracious love, the more that grace can pour into our hearts. In process thought, I see what always made sense to me: that more grace means more freedom, more human responsibility, more "works"; and more "works" allow more grace.

Summary

Chapter 3 provided a distinction in the idea of change. We saw that God is unchanging in the sense that God loves the world perfectly. But for that very reason, the expressions of God's love are constantly changing in response to the decisions and needs of the world.

Now we can say the same thing about God's knowledge. It is an unchanging structure of God's nature that God always knows everything there is to know. But what exists for God to know—the decisions of the creatures—is constantly changing, constantly becoming. In this sense, precisely because God unchangeably knows everything there is to know, God's knowledge is constantly changing. While you and I are only partially aware of a tiny fraction of the events of this vast universe, God is fully aware of all those events in each new moment. So our knowledge is finite and partial, changing only imperfectly in response to the world, while God's knowledge is infinite, changing perfectly in response to the world.

Process theologians would say that God has eternally had perfect and unchanging knowledge of all the *possibilities* for the world. But because the world has real freedom to choose between those possibilities, God's knowledge of the actual choices made is constantly changing as the world changes.

Actually, this is a very biblical view of God. In the Old Testament especially, the prophets constantly confront people with choices. If you repent and obey God's call, God will be able to bless you. If you sin and rebel against God, God will punish you. In process theology God does not control the world so easily as the biblical view would suggest. But process theologians affirm that the biblical vision of our freedom to choose is true and that God awaits our choice.

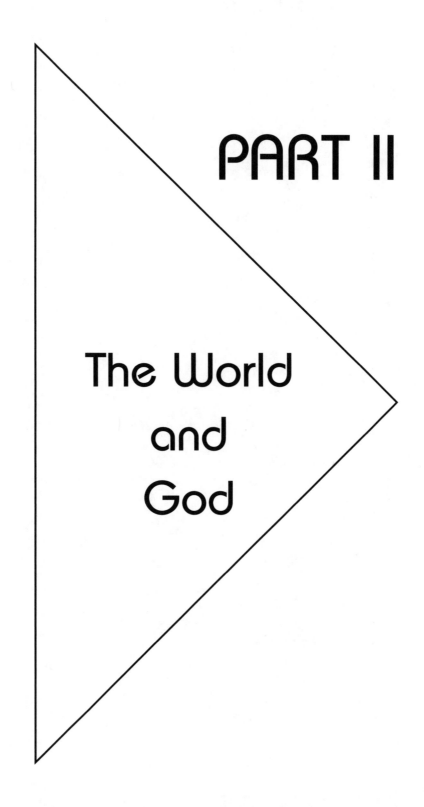

PART II

The World
and
God

Introduction
to Part II

How does God act in the world? Most theologies have no answer to this question other than to deny that one is needed. God is said to be supernatural, to be above the laws of nature and hence not bound by them. God can simply do whatever God wants to do. This has satisfied most people for a long time. But for people who think very seriously today, it satisfies less and less.

The great world religions emerged prior to the rise of modern science, in times when we had no idea at all how nature worked. Having no notion of natural laws or processes, no one thought of God as violating them. Until very recently, most people believed (and some still do) that the sun rises because God tells it to, that rain falls because God opens the windows of heaven and lets in the water that is above the dome of the sky, that women become barren or fertile because

God so wills it. The Bible expresses each of these beliefs repeatedly.

Today we know better. The sun "rises" and "sets" because the earth revolves on its axis. What, then, does God have to do with it? As we have learned more about nature, we have seen less and less for God to do. Indeed, there has been little room in the chain of natural causes for God to play any role at all. Since there are always things we do not yet know, people have tended to use God to plug the gaps in our knowledge. If we don't know how nature does something then we say, "God did it." But as we close the gaps in our knowledge this "God of the gaps" becomes smaller, hiding in the shadows of our ignorance, hiding from the light of knowledge. Such theologies inevitably make scientific knowledge and open inquiry the enemies of faith and of God. It is a pitiful picture of God.

One of the great virtues of process theology is its ability to offer views of God and the world that hang together, that accept and build on what we know of nature through scientific investigation. When process theologians are asked how God acts in the world they have an answer that does not escape into the supernatural world of magic and wishful thinking, but embraces the scientific quest for knowledge and all that it teaches us.

It is not only science, of course, that raises these questions for us. We need no special science to show us the diversity of world religions, the impact of history and culture on scripture and revelation, the tragedies of human oppression, and the myriad ways in which the world kills and maims humans and other animals. Yet these are important features of the world for which our theology must be able to account.

To believe in the supernatural God of the tradition we must abandon the quest to understand the world on its own natural terms. That is too high a price. To understand how the God of process theology acts we need only open our minds to a new vision of the world.

In this section I have tried to summarize basic features of the process vision of the world and God as simply as possible. Naturally, many questions will be left unanswered. But I hope that it will provide enough background to make the rest of the book intelligible and to give readers a sense of the excitement and wonder that have drawn me to process thought.

CHAPTER 5

Time

Begin with your own experience. What is it like? One obvious and inescapable feature of all experience is that it continually becomes. You can't hold it still.

As a child traveling to my grandparents' home for Christmas I watched the reflectors along the highway at night. I would focus my eyes on one ahead of us as we approached it at 60 mph. I kept trying to freeze that moment when the reflector was neither before or behind me, but right along side. I always failed. I could anticipate its coming, see it beside me, and recall that moment to my mind as memory. But the actual moment would never hold still. It came and went. Even if the car stopped beside one, that moment of finally stopping would never hold still. Maneuver as we will, the momentary "now" will elude capture. It will slip through our fingers more surely than any wave on a beach or breeze on our hand.

We can savor moments, but even the savoring involves a series of moments that refuse to stand still for us. We can anticipate moments in advance, or remember them after the fact. But moments become and perish.

This does not mean that the present moment is an illusion, while only the past and future are real. Instead, the present moment holds it all. The past "exists" as a memory in the present moment. The future "exists" as a range of possibilities latent in the present moment. Yet the phrase *present moment* has a shifting meaning like the word *today*. We are always "in the present," but the present is a continually shifting ground. It won't hold still for us.

Process thinkers believe that what is true of our personal experience is true of all of reality. Your experience of this moment did not exist (was possible but not actual) just a moment ago. Each new moment or event of your experience becomes and then perishes, making way for a new event of experience. In the same way (though infinitely more complex) the myriad events constituting the entire universe come into existence in each moment and then perish, making way for new events that were never actual before. The universe is new in each moment, just as your experience is new.

Connectedness

Yet, despite being continually new, you and the universe "hang together" with amazing stubbornness. The present moment is connected with the past. Imagine a friend suddenly giving you a big hug. The feelings and thoughts you have in the next moments will arise out of that experience of being hugged. What is more, you will feel those feelings as arising out of the earlier feelings. You experience causal connections. These *connections* are not themselves experienced by our senses, but by an intrinsic character of feeling the present feelings (of feeling loved, or perhaps embarrassed) as arising out of previous feelings (of being hugged). The same principle could be tested with anger, frustration, or literally any experience at all. We experience the present as arising out of the past.

Just as we experience present feelings as arising out of previous ones, we anticipate future events arising out of present ones. We experience our present decisions as setting the stage for future possibilities, as providing the raw materials out of which we expect some future events to be created. Thus you are reading this sentence now with the expectation that it will play some role in your later thinking.

Life is inescapably lived out in present moments that we experience as arising out of our past and as preparing the way for a range of possible futures. Memory and anticipation are our human expressions for those causal connections that we directly experience between moments of time. The world hangs together with enormous continuity over time, and is usually pretty predictable. The past largely determines the future.

Freedom

Yet determinism is not all that we experience. There are also unexpected leaps and shifts. We surprise others and even ourselves by changing our minds, by suddenly striking out in new directions, by singing in a new key. Of the options open to us, we sometimes choose an unlikely one, or perhaps find unexpected options opened to us by unforeseen events. The world contains chance and freedom as well as determinism.

Of course, even our freedom itself arises out of the past. I am not free to change the past. Rather, what I am free to do right now is a result of the past. Having spent many years in graduate school, I am free to walk into my classroom and either lecture, lead a discussion, or give a quiz. By contrast, I am surrounded here in Iowa by people who have spent their whole lives learning how to turn soil and seed into an abundant harvest. My past choices have not prepared me to do what they can do. The ranges of our freedoms are not the same. And having made our decisions to be in southern Iowa right now, neither the farmers nor I are free to be in Africa one minute from now. Our past both creates and limits our options.

Process thinkers believe that the universe hangs together in the same way your own experience does—except that most events in the universe are less creative than those in your mind. The event that is the present moment for an electron is almost entirely a repetition of the events of the immediate past of that electron. Electrons just aren't very creative. And so the events of the "material" universe in each moment arise out of past events with much greater stability and persistence, and much less creativity than do the events of your own experience. In fact, the universe has enormous inertia, an enormous drive toward continuing the past. Hence, a stable world.

Yet even electrons, we know, are not entirely determined by the past. The amazing thing about modern physics is the persistent evidence that no matter what you do to control an electron (or other elementary—individual—"particles") it will have more than one possible response. It can go in more than one direction, behave in more than one way, make more than one "choice."

Is an electron free? It isn't free to fall in love, to be angry, to write poetry, or to taste lemonade. The important aspects of human freedom are irrelevant to electrons. But there is one sense in which electrons and human minds may both be said to be free. Given a set of conditions they can respond in more than one way. And that is the root meaning of freedom. In this sense, process thinkers see in modern physics a world in which freedom is a basic fact of reality.

If the material world is free in this very negligible sense, can a bullet decide not to shatter a person's chest? No.

First of all, the freedom of the individual electrons, protons, and neutrons composing the bullet is trivial. They respond only to the physical fields of which they are parts. They do not have sense organs to see the chest, or brains with which to anticipate and evaluate the consequences of their actions. They only choose "this way" or "that way." And bullets are not like people. They do not have nervous systems that organize and integrate all of the individual experiences into one mind that can act for the whole. Bullets just go, blindly and uncaringly, and so does most of the world. Freedom may be inherent in the building blocks of the world, but it only becomes significant when those blocks are organized in very special ways.

Secondly, when we deal with such elementary entities, which are not organized so as to give rise to any higher form of experience, statistical laws take over. Even when one or a few entities make decisions other than the norm, they are simply overwhelmed by their neighbors. As physicists frequently observe, we cannot predict what a single electron will do, but we can predict with incredible accuracy what a bullet will do, because sheer statistics overpower individual decisions.

The organization of the world to allow higher experience will be the topic of the next chapter. For now, let us return to the question of time and the becoming of the universe.

Time and Eternity

People have often sought for some enduring, permanent, unchanging, eternal ground underneath what Plato called the "perpetual perishing" of time. Plato, for example, thought that what was "really real" was timeless Being, while the physical world of Becoming was a mere shadowy appearance. Christianity and many other visions of reality have shared this intuition that Being is more fundamental than Becoming.

Process thinkers see no timeless Being underneath the reality of Becoming. We believe time is the passage of events, and only that. To look for something beneath the events as the true nature of time or reality is simply to miss the point. Our experience is inescapably composed of this passage. It is our reality. It is within this continual flow of events that we live, and move, and have our being. It is in the becoming of events that we love and care and grow and find whatever meaning and joy there is for us. The passage of events is what there is.

God and Time

God shares this adventure of time, according to process theists. In Chapter 4 we have already seen that their belief in freedom leads process theologians to reject the idea that God lives in a timeless eternity or sees all of time as equally actual and present. The conclusion is that time is as real for God as for us. And yet, there certainly are ways in which process theologians see God's experience of time as different from ours.

First, God's view of time is different because God is everlasting (though not timeless). That is, God has always existed and always will exist. God cannot grow old or die. Time does not threaten God as it does us.

Second, there are features of God's existence that, as we have already seen, are unchangeable. It is an unchangeable fact that God is perfectly loving, that God knows everything there is to know, that God is always doing everything within God's power to work for the good. Especially, God has a "primordial nature," which is God's knowledge of all possibilities. Most process theologians agree with Whitehead that possibilities are eternal; they may be more or less relevant and they may or may not be actualized in any given moment. But what is or will be possible always was possible. And since God knows all there is to know, God has eternally and unchangeably known all the infinite realm of possiblity. And it is this fact about God that ultimately makes novelty and freedom possible in the world.

It is precisely these unchanging facts that necessarily involve God in the adventure of time. For God's love, knowledge, and activity are constantly responsive to events in the world. For God shares the experience of every event in the universe. God shares the "experience" of every electron, every amoeba, every individual living cell in every living plant and animal. God shares the experience of every worm, ant, bat, dog, whale, and person. And if there are living things elsewhere in the universe, God shares their experience, too. God shares the experience of becoming of the entire universe, and synthesizes it into God's own, infinitely vast and complex experience.

God and the universe are co-eternal. God always has existed and always will exist. And in some form the world always has existed and always will. There was never a time (or a timeless eternity) when God was not creatively working. Nor will there ever be a time (or timeless eternity) when God ceases to act creatively in the world. The universe as we know it probably began and will end in a "Big Bang," but this is only one episode in the infinite history of time. God has shared and will share the adventure of time forever. However we may wish to speak of a "reign of God," it will not, in process theology, mean the end of time or of God's creative activity.

The world, then, is like the jazz combo in the sense that the "music" is not eternally frozen onto a record. It is coming into existence in each moment.

CHAPTER 6

A World of Experience

The one thing any of us can be sure of is our own experience. We *know* we experience. Yet we seem surrounded by a material world devoid of experience—desks, rocks, trees, fountain pens. How could such a world as that give birth to such creatures as ourselves? Indeed, how are we to understand our relationships to our own bodies if they are made up of nonexperiencing matter? To see human souls as supernatural beings injected into this world by God has comforted many, but leaves modern thinkers increasingly unsatisfied. Are we not parts of nature, emerging from and depending upon the world about us? Are we not closely akin to the other animals who seem to feel their own pleasures and pains? How are we to understand the place of minds in nature?

51

To answer such questions, we must explore the ways in which process thinkers see the world as composed entirely of events of experience. Once we grasp this vision, we may be able to have some understanding of the process vision of how God acts in the world, of what God can and cannot do, and of why process theology takes the fate of the natural environment, including animals, so seriously.

Humans and Other Animals

We know that we have experience. Strictly speaking, of course, I only assume that you have experience. I assume it because you are so much like me. You have eyes and nerve cells and a spinal cord and a brain like mine. And you act very much like I act when we both touch something hot or sharp. We have good reasons for believing that other people have experiences very much like our own.

What of other animals? (I say other animals because we, of course, are animals, too.)

Most Christians have believed that human souls are created supernaturally by God. Christians have usually held that we are in this natural world but not *of* it. Rather, we are set within it in order to have dominion over it. Not surprisingly, some Christians have held that since God creates human souls supernaturally, other animals must have no souls and so must not have experience. They must feel no pain; they are only robots that squeak when damaged. Consequently, we need have no concern for their welfare or worry about their suffering. This theology has had devastating consequences for animals, the environment, and ultimately for us as well.

The view that only humans have experience seems arrogant and foolish given the tremendous extent to which higher animals are like us. Dogs and cats and monkeys have eyes and nerve cells and spinal cords and even brains very much like ours. Their brains lack important sections dealing with abstract thought, but include sections dealing with pain, fear, and other emotions. They react to heat and sharp objects, to food and kind words, very much like people do. We have good reason to believe that while dogs and cats cannot do abstract math, cannot engage in moral discourse, and cannot write poetry, they can feel pain, hunger, fear, and affection.

Apes, whales, and dolpins are even more intriguing to us. Their behavior often seems to be more human than that of dogs or cats. Koko, an ape, became famous for learning sign language and for having a pet kitten. Whales seem to communicate through a means we feel compelled to call "singing." Their songs are tremendously complex, showing variations over time. Perhaps they write poetry of their own kind.

In varying degrees, other animals appear to intend actions, anticipate events in the near future, and feel some degree of sympathy for others. Also, it is worth noting that we lack a dolphin's ability to "see" the world accoustically and to communicate that sonic image to others. So even if we say that (most?) other animals don't think abstractly in our manner, some animals certainly do a lot that might be called thinking.

We can never know what it is like to be another person. But we are confident that it is like something. In the same way, we cannot know what it is like to be a bat or whale, but surely it is like something.

Still, it does appear that some kinds of thought occur in human minds that are (probably) not present in the minds of other animals. High levels of abstraction and moral reflection are among forms of consciousness that seem to be (probably) unique to humans on this planet. Going "down" the animal kingdom means to us finding animals less and less like ourselves. Their nervous systems and brains are less like ours. Yet, there is powerful evidence that bees have intricate means of chemical communication and complex social structures. So far as we can tell they lack the kinds of brains necessary to do abstract math or moral thinking. Yet are we prepared to deny that they have some experiences of pleasure and pain and behave in socially significant ways?

What of simple organisms that lack central nervous systems and brains altogether? What of single living cells?

We have compelling reason to believe that as we move "down" the animal kingdom the experiences of living creatures become less and less complex. Abstract thinking disappears first, along with some forms of emotions that depend on our ability to foresee the far future. Then, other emotions and intentionality are lost as brains become smaller. Probably consciousness depends upon a central nervous system.

Sense experiences are present but different from ours—as in bats using sonar or snakes sensing body heat. Gradually even sense experience is lost as we move toward animals without eyes, ears, or tongues. Yet they still have ways of finding their way to food. How does an amoeba find food? I don't know. Yet it reacts to the world about it in very simple, yet fascinating ways.

If there is any sense at all in saying that amoebas have experience—however primitive, however remote from our own—then what of plants? Plants lack brains, nerve cells, sense organs like ours and central nervous systems. Yet perhaps their individual cells still have very low levels of unconscious experience, and perhaps they even share their experience in ways we cannot imagine.

The "Material" World

Finally, if we have not thrown up our hands at such nonsense long ago, what of electrons? Do they have experience? Surely they can have none of the experiences that depend upon the incredibly complex organization of living cells. If we can even bring ourselves to stretch the word *experience* so far as to include electrons, they can probably be said to experience only their spatial/temporal relationships with other subatomic events around them, so that their experiences would be what physicists mean when they talk of the physical fields constituting the material world of space and time, as well as the range of possible responses they may have to those relationships.

If we allow that dogs have experience, we have stretched that word beyond its ordinary human use. But how many of us would refuse to do so? If we say that bats have experience we stretch the word even further. If we include bees as having experience we have already pushed the word far beyond its normal bounds. But isn't there some reason to do so? And if, finally, we say that electrons have experience of spacial/temporal relationships, which constitute the physical universe, we have come to think of the entire universe as a world of pure experience, with electrons (or perhaps quarks) at one end of a spectrum and ourselves (so far as we know) at the other. (Though perhaps the universe is filled with creatures as far beyond us as we are beyond dogs.)

At their end of the spectrum of experience, electrons may be said to have experience that is almost purely physical. Such experience would not involve consciousness, of course. Even lower animals seem to lack that. It would have nothing to do with passions, ideas, or morality. The only sense in which they might be said to have conceptual experience would be their capacity to "decide" between moving this way or that way. This constitutes their whole realm of freedom.

This does not mean that rocks or tables or fountain pens have souls. In ordinary physical objects there is no experience above the level of the individual particles, or perhaps the molecules, composing them. That is true of most of the universe. Most of the universe is made of events of experience of energy fields, of spatial-temporal relationships. Since such experiences mainly repeat the events before them, there is plenty of stubborn stability and order in the world.

Nevertheless, every individual in the universe has some capacity to create itself. Every electron-event encounters some small range of possible ways in which it might become in the present moment. And as electrons join with other elementary individuals into atoms and molecules and finally into living cells, they give rise to creatures for whom experience becomes more complex and more intense, with a wider range of possible responses to the world. As living cells are arranged into bodies with nervous systems, eyes, ears, and brains, experience becomes so incredibly rich and complex that the wealth of experience of billions of individuals can be amplified, transformed, and fed into a single, central experience capable not only of physical feelings like pain, pleasure, and hunger, but also of thought and imagination, and of emotions like love, hate, and jealously, which combine physical feelings with thought. Given all of these complexities, there arises the capacity for moral thought and significant moral freedom.

A Relational World

If you recall the discussion of Chapter 3, you will remember the implications of viewing the world in terms of "substances," which endure unchanged through change, and which require only themselves in order to exist. In contrast, process thinkers see the world as fundamentally relational, coming into existence anew in each moment, and building itself out of its past.

Think again of your own experience. In each moment you create yourself. But you do not create yourself out of nothing. Rather, you create yourself out of everything that has gone before. When someone insults you and makes you angry, the anger of that moment is felt in the next moment, but from a new point of view. *We literally feel the feelings of past events, but they are now transformed by being set in a new relationship.*

As a simple analogy think of a snowball. Obviously there isn't any snowball apart from the snow and other bits of gravel and grass and leaves that form the ball. We don't first have the "true snowball," apart from any snow at all, and then begin to add snow. There is no snowball other than the "togetherness" of the stuff of which it is made. The same is true of everything in the world, including human souls. Each momentary event in the enduring series of experiences we call our mind or soul is a bundle of experienced relationships. Take away the experienced relations and nothing is left.

Recently I told my wife that she was in my soul—and I meant it. For over twenty years my relationship with her has been of paramount importance in my decisions about how I will create myself. She and I have shaped each other. Decisions that she makes about who she will be and how she will act call forth responses in me. I experience her, and then create myself by deciding who I will be—how I will act. Her love and anger and joy and frustration express themselves in ways that I experience, experiences that are literally part of who I am. And it is by taking those experiences in and deciding how I will respond to them that I create myself. Her life is literally part of my life. Without her I would be a different person than I am—probably a profoundly different person.

What is true of my relationship with Barbara—that I create myself out of that relationship—is true, in varying degrees of importance, of my relation to everything and everyone else in the world. If there had been no big bang twenty billion years ago I would not be here. If stars billions of years away in time and space had not exploded and spewed forth their gifts of heavy elements, I would not be here. My life is a product of all that has gone before. Though I respond consciously and thoughtfully to only a tiny portion of the universe, it all touches me. I do not first exist and then have relationships. I am who I am because of the relationships of which I am a part, because of the decisions other creatures make about how to create themselves, and because of the decisions I make about how to respond to my relationships with them.

Because I am a finite person, I can only sustain a very few conscious and central relationships. Because I am emotionally limited I find it hard to sustain relationships of love with those who hate me or who are far away. Because I am finite in intelligence and security I find it difficult to understand and acknowledge the vast range of relationships that form my life. But they are all there, whether I know it or not.

When we impoverish others, we impoverish ourselves. When we enrich the lives of others, we enrich ourselves. For we create ourselves out of them.

Process theologians say that when we impoverish others we also impoverish God, for the divine life, too, is continually sharing the lives of all. It is possible to add and substract from infinity, to add more to it or less. God's life is infinitely rich; yet, God shares the life of the world, of my wife, my children, me, and you. Had we made better decisions, we could have contributed greater richness to God. We could have given God more with which to work in God's ongoing effort to bring about good.

What is true of our relationships with other people is true of our relationships with all creatures and God. We create ourselves out of our relationships with them. We had better have a care about the world in which we live.

CHAPTER 7

How God Acts in the World

If process theologians are correct, this is a world of experience, and every experience includes an experience of God. The experience of God's love is the foundation of reality, say process theologians. What does this mean?

God as the Foundation of Freedom

To be free an individual must have a range of possibilities from which to choose. Process theologians see God's "primordial nature," God's eternal experience of all possibilities, as the foundation of the freedom of the world. Every creature in every moment experiences God. We experience God in that we experience the range of possibilities relevant to this moment of our existence. Process theologians say that we also experience God's "lure" toward some of those possibilities over others. By providing possibilities in a context of values, God enters into the experience of every creature in every moment in the infinite history of the universe, making freedom and values possible.

In different words, every creature experiences God's loving care for its moment of creativity. Each creative moment is born in God's creative love. Without that divine spark the world could not become. Thus when process theologians affirm that all of reality is grounded in God's love, they mean it with full seriousness. And the most basic expression of God's love is that God acts as the ground of creaturely freedom.

God Cannot Overrule Freedom

Most Christians would say that while God may give us our freedom, God is also able to overrule it whenever God wishes. They say, however, that God obviously chooses to refrain from such intrusion in most cases so as to allow us freedom. The underlying assumption being that freedom is a gift so great that it is worth the price of all the suffering it makes possible. Some Christians today might extend this idea to say that God has made an eternal blanket choice not to overrule human freedom, and God obviously won't go back on such a choice. Either way, when the problem of evil arises, either of these constitutes what is commonly called the "freewill defense" of God's failure to prevent suffering. Process theology, in contrast, is saying quite starkly that God cannot overrule creaturely freedom.

The moral differences between process theology and the "freewill defense" become obvious when we ask why God fails to overrule the freedom of a toddler about to walk out in front of a car. We would not accept the freewill defense from human parents who failed to protect that endangered toddler, so why should we accept it as a view of God?

Process theologians agree that God is the ground of freedom, but they do not think of freedom as something that God might simply choose to withhold or overrule. Why not?

Process theologians believe that freedom is an inherent feature of reality. The universe is the becoming of events that are self-creative, from quarks to human minds. Without freedom there would be no world. Freedom is not a gift that God controls or that God could withdraw and still have any world at all. "No freedom" means "no creatures."

In one sense, then, freedom is simply a brute fact about the world that even God cannot destroy. But there is another sense in which God actively works to "give us" our agency. And that is through the evolutionary process. After we understand how God must work in the world to evolve creatures as free as human beings, we will see why God cannot simply override that work in a single moment.

God and Evolution

Imagine a few trillion gamma particles zipping about the earth four billion years ago. These particles are largely determined by their environment, but like all elementary ("individual") events they have some trivial capacity to respond to their physical environment in more than one way. Perhaps if some of them were to go "this way" rather than "that way" they might strike some primitive living cells and generate mutations, giving the evolutionary process of natural selection more novel material with which to work. A process theologian might see God's hand in the evolutionary process partly as "calling" those gamma particles "this way" in the hopes that a few will respond and nudge the evolutionary process along toward more interesting possibilities.

Process theologians would see God as working patiently through the evolutionary process to bring into existence new kinds of creatures with greater levels of freedom. An electron's experience of God is trivial. Within an organic molecule, an electron has a richer set of relationships to experience. As those molecules combine with others in appropriate ways, there arise organisms with substantially greater capacities for novel response to their environment. While biologists would have more precise definitions, it is important to see that part of what we mean by "life" is this very capacity for novelty. The biologist's definition will point to those features of an organism that make this creativity possible.

Compared to an electron or an organic molecule, an amoeba's freedom is vastly greater, and its experience of God is correspondingly richer. Yet, compared to whales or apes or humans, an amoeba's experience is incredibly trivial. God and evolution still had a long way to go to produce creatures with lives we might think of as interesting. But whales and apes and human beings could not be created by God without all of the rest of the biological network upon which we depend. There had to be a universe of electrons, oceans of plankton, jungles full of bananas, and a whole ecological system before there could be whales or apes or us.

It has taken God billions of years to draw the world through an evolutionary process capable of sustaining human beings. The freedom we enjoy is founded on a whole world of creatures. The freedom of our minds depends upon and arises out of the experience of the billions of cells that form our bodies at any moment. It is simply not within God's power to overturn all of that in a single moment.

We have bodies with hands that can reach out and pull a trigger or grab a child. God does not. So we can overrule each other's freedom in ways God cannot. God is everywhere and everytime. God can make freedom possible for an entire universe, moving it through an evolutionary process to create a universe of experience. We cannot. We are only here and now. Our powers are ours, not God's. And God's powers are God's, not ours. God cannot overrule our freedom.

God gives us our freedom as a gift in the sense that God has worked through billions of years to create a world capable of producing creatures with brains and bodies so complex that they can produce minds like ours, capable of great freedom. Perhaps God might have chosen not to do this at all—though it seems unlikely. God must share responsibility with the world for our existence, for our ability to be kind and cruel. But now that we are here, we must accept responsibility for what we do. God cannot save us from ourselves or from the rest of the world upon which we depend.

Humans, Other Creatures, and God

Now we come to another important difference between process thought and traditional theologies. Process theologians do not assume that human beings are the center or end of God's creative activity. God's creative activity extends infinitely into the past and will continue into an infinite future. We and our world are only here for a brief moment in that infinity. God's love and God's plans do not begin and end with us.

Furthermore, since God cannot control the evolutionary process, there is no reason even to assume that God was aiming that process specifically at us. The history of evolution has been filled with more crucial events than we can dream of, and God could not control them. God and the world have been involved in a continuous dance in which God must continually take the decisions of the creatures and work with them—whatever they may be. For better or worse, each decision of each creature plays some role in the world's process of becoming. And God works to create something good out of what the world makes possible.

Evolution, then, is an ongoing adventure for God, as it is for the world. We need not suppose that God has some specific species, like humans, or some specific social structure, like American capitalism, as a divine goal. Rather, we should say that God aims at richness of experience, both for God and the world. God shares the experience of every creature. So the pleasure and pain of bees, bats, and baboons are part of God's life. Their lives matter to God. So if we care for God's life we should care for theirs.

Process theology demands that we stop seeing the happiness of human beings as the sole purpose of God's existence and creative activity. We must respect all of creation and all the other creatures with whom we share this world, for they also have their enjoyments and they also contribute to God's life. The pain of animals in the laboratory, the misery of life in a small wire cage, and the agony of a fox in a steel trap are shared by God just as much as the misery of human beings.

Nevertheless, there are ways in which humans play a role in God's life that lower animals cannot. At the level of human beings—where experience becomes so rich and complex that it crosses the crucial boundary into consciousness, into abstractions, into the ability to anticipate the distant future and consider a wide range of complex possibilities—moral freedom becomes possible and our experience of God becomes dramatically more important. Human beings can experience possibilities of great moral importance, along with God's call to choose some rather than others. We can experience depths of love and joy and sharing that are probably impossible for lower animals on our planet.

Of course, we can only barely imagine what other creatures there may be in this vast universe. There may be creatures with levels of experience so far beyond our own that their contributions to God's life are much greater than ours, and their experience of God comparably richer than ours. If the process theologians' vision of divinity is correct, then we must assume that God's creative work is not limited to our small species in this enormous cosmos.

God is not a human being. Surely we are not the center or end of God's universe or God's creativity. There may be creatures in the universe who enjoy a far deeper communion with God than we can. And we may evolve into creatures far better and more complex than we are now.

This does not mean that God does not love us. Life is not a competition for God's love. God's love is infinite, touching all creatures in their kind. God's love enters into each moment of our lives just as it enters into the lives of all creatures everywhere.

The Interweaving of God and the World

Our experience of God is interwoven with our experience of the entire past universe. Our own past decisions and our immediate environment affect us the most. They create the situations that make possibilities more or less relevant. If someone has punched me in the nose, my response will be shaped by my whole past life. If I am a fighter I'll probably hit back. If I have worked to avoid violence I will probably look for some other option. But whatever my past, there will be more than one possible response, and there will be some responses more productive of good than others. My experience of God is my experience of those possibilities along with God's call toward the better ones.

Sometimes, of course, even the best possibilities are bad, and this is a fact God cannot change. If I have just fired a bullet at someone, God cannot change that fact. God cannot stop the bullet. And even the best options God can share with me are pretty terrible.

Can God work with the material world apart from evolution? Since rocks and bullets are not individuals with their own experience, and since malaria mosquitos are not capable of considering the consequences of their feeding on human blood, there is not much God can do to influence them. But there are some things God can do.

Imagine diseased cells in a human body. Mostly these cells will operate according to fixed patterns and they are quite incapable of having feelings of sympathy for the larger human organism of which they are parts. Of course, there are healthy cells in the body working to bring about healing. If we see the human mind as intrinsically a part of the human body, and learn that it is one experiencer among others in the body, we may learn how the mind and God can cooperate in assisting those healthier cells in their work. And if such assistance is successful, it would not be a miraculous suspension of natural law. Nor would it be that God had decided to cure this person rather than the millions of others. God continually calls the world and us toward the best, but it is up to the world to respond.

God has no supernatural power to coerce the world. But God does work in the world for health and healing. Given the difference between cancer cells and human minds, God's best avenue to bring about health in the world is by calling people to learn how to heal themselves. And indeed, we can hardly overlook the amazing miracles of modern medicine. But process theologians would not rule out altogether the possibility that bodily cells might also, on some occasions, suprise us with their responsiveness to God's call toward health. Nor should we be surprised to learn that our minds and bodies interact more and have more power to heal each other than we now know.

Finally, God works in the world by being responsive. God shares the experience of every momentary creature. God shares the experience of electrons and gamma particles, of bats, and whales, and people. God takes in the experience of the world and responds with options and callings appropriate to our past decisions and present situations.

The world ends up rather like a jazz combo, after all. Each creature creates itself with some degree of freedom shaped by the "music" that has already been played and the whispered suggestions of God toward more beautiful harmonies and contrasts. But the music does not exist until the creatures create it. And whatever melody God may have in mind, it is up to the creatures to do the playing.

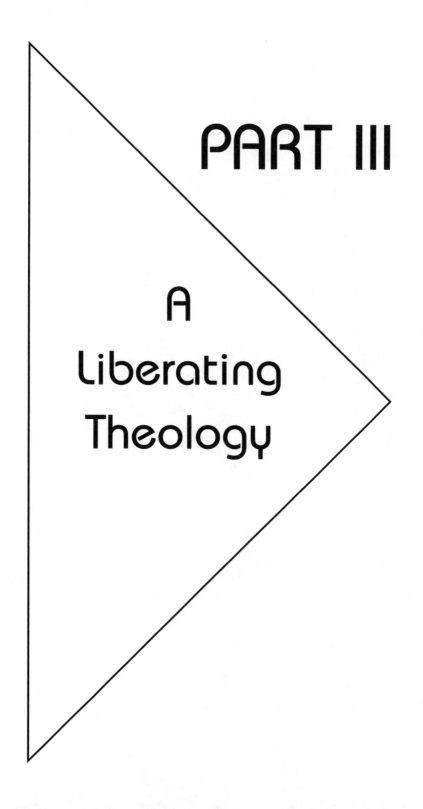

PART III

A
Liberating
Theology

Introduction
to Part III

Whenever I write theology or philosophy, I struggle with the question of whether it will only distract readers from the truly important questions that confront us. On the one hand these questions regard the many sources of misery in our world—disease, poverty, sexism, militarism, racism, etc.— and such threats to our planetary life as nuclear weapons, overpopulation, and pollution. On the other hand, there are truly important questions about how we can best care for our own children and loved ones right now, this very day.

In all honesty, I think that questions about how to work for human liberation and the welfare of the planet are more important than questions about the nature of God, and so would many process theologians. Surely the God of process theology would be anxious for us to focus on the problems affecting our survival. But it is a fact that what we believe about God shapes our responses to these other issues. There is certainly much of value in the traditional image of God as Father. But if we believe that God *is* "Father," that the Father commands women to remain silent in the church, and that the present system of male dominance exists because it is part of the Father's eternal plan as described in the Bible, then we are going to oppose the move toward greater equality for women.

Other images, however, can open us up to richly and excitingly different spiritual journeys. Sally McFague has suggested the images of God as Mother, Lover, and Friend. Shug, in Alice Walker's *The Color Purple*, suggests, "Conjure up flowers, wind, water, a big rock." The Christian tradition of God's omnipresence affirms that there is no dimension of reality that cannot be the occasion for revealing the divine. We need to explore images that help us open up to the many faces of the sacred. Especially we need images that pull us beyond narrow visions of who and what is important and toward larger visions of liberation for all.

Given these convictions about what is important and how theology affects our attitudes toward vital questions, I want to frame this section of the book so that these connections are at the center.

There is a clear risk involved. My primary goal is to present a positive vision that draws people toward something good rather than just negatively attacking existing ideas. But if being positive means being afraid to be honest about the serious problems I see in traditional theologies, the strategy would be self-defeating. And besides, any thoughtful reader is going to see the negative implications of my positive vision anyway, so I might as well bring them out into the open where they can be considered in their proper place. Please remember that my final goal is not merely to tear down, but to offer constructive alternatives.

CHAPTER 8

How Religion Becomes Oppressive

About 580 B.C., the Greek philosopher Xenophanes observed that "if cattle or lions had hands, so as to paint with their hands and produce works of art as men do, they would paint their gods and give them bodies in form like their own—horses like horses, cattle like cattle." His point, of course, was not about animals, but about us. We, too, paint God—both on walls and in our minds—as if God were like us.

Ludwig Feuerbach, a nineteenth century German philosopher, pushed this idea further, saying that theology is really anthropology. When we study the gods of any culture, we are really studying the people. The values of the people are projected outside themselves into the gods they worship. Warrior tribes, for example, are likely to have warrior gods. Gods, of course, are more than human. So human values are not merely projected onto gods, but are magnified. The warrior god will be much stronger and fiercer than human warriors.[1]

Of course, we are not usually conscious that we are doing this. We do not think of our gods or their values as projections of ourselves. We assume that our pictures of the gods are accurate images of divine reality, of eternal truth and goodness.

Since we human beings are often filled with conflicting feelings about what we value, it should not be surprising that our gods reflect and magnify these conflicts. Consider, for example, the God of traditional Christianity who is said to love all persons infinitely and unconditionally. Here, surely, we see the highest of our values raised to its ultimate. And yet, we can easily see how our human narrowness and vengefulness infect our theology when we remember that Christians usually have described God as casting the majority of human beings into eternal hellfire for failing to believe in a religion of which they had never heard. Indeed, Christians have generally believed that their God predestines people to burn in hell for sins they were predestined to commit. The terrible result of all this is that sending people to hell becomes seen as an expression of divine love!

The traditional Christian belief that all Jews automatically go to hell has made it easy for Christians to view them as enemies of God who not only may, but should, be punished for being Jewish. The Nazi concentrations camps were just an extension of this theology.

Another concrete and tragic example of this merger of conflicting values, which has contributed to centuries of misery for slaves of Christian masters, can be found in 1 Peter 2:18–21. For years I quoted verses 21–24 as one of my favorite expressions of how the crucified Christ calls Christians to be

---

[1]There are obvious ways in which process theology reflects contemporary American thought and culture. This does not automatically invalidate it any more than any theory is invalidated by reflecting the best current thinking. This ability to respond intelligently to the most severe contemporary challenges and to reflect the very best of modern thought is surely a strength of process theology. But process thinkers are certainly aware of Whitehead's humbling comment that I cited in the introduction to this book: "There remains the final reflection, how shallow, puny, and imperfect are efforts to sound the depths in the nature of things. In philosophical discussion, the merest hint of dogmatic certainty as to finality of statement is an exhibition of folly." (Preface to *Process and Reality: An Essay in Cosmology*, [The Free Press, corrected edition, Griffin and Sherburne, editors, 1978], p. xiv.)

models of sacrificial love. Then one day I began reading at verse 18 and was horrified at what I saw.

> [18]Slaves must be respectful and obedient to their masters, not only when they are kind and gentle but also when they are unfair. [19]You see, there is some merit in putting up with the pains of unearned punishment if it is done for the sake of God [20]but there is nothing meritorious in taking a beating patiently if you have done something wrong to deserve it. The merit, in the sight of God, is in bearing it patiently when you are punished after doing your duty.

> [21]This, in fact, is what you were called to do, because Christ suffered for you and left an example for you to follow. (JB)

A very similar passage can be found in 1 Timothy 6:1–2:

> [1]All slaves "under the yoke" must have unqualified respect for their masters, so that the name of God and our teaching are not brought into disrepute. Slaves whose masters are believers are not to think any the less of them because [2]they are brothers; on the contrary, they should serve them all the better, since those who have the benefit of their services are believers and dear to God.(JB)[2]

The tragedy is that Christ became, partially, a projection of the values of slave owners. Jesus, like Yahweh in the Old Testament, was used to sanction slavery and to command obedience in slaves. Thus the very worst and most selfish of human values, as well as the highest and best, can be projected into our images of God.

We must see clearly what happens here. Human beings have values that are shaped by their culture and personal

---

[2]Although written in the names of Peter and Paul, nonfundamentalist New Testament scholars very widely agree that 1 Peter and 1 Timothy were in fact written by authors in the 2nd century A.D. Paul himself once said that in Christ "there is no longer slave or free" (Galatians 3:28), and his letter to Philemon has powerful antislavery sentiment. Regretfully, his belief that Jesus would return soon caused him to say that slaves should not be concerned with seeking their freedom. "Let each of you lead the life that the Lord has assigned, to which God has called you....Were you a slave when called? Do not be concerned about it." See 1 Corinthians 7:17–32.

experience. People who have the most power in a society and benefit from it the most—who are fairly wealthy, free, and happy—will naturally see their society as good. Meanwhile, those who are the powerless victims of a society—the slaves, the impoverished, the exploited, the oppressed—will naturally have a different view.

Unconsciously, those with power in a society will shape their gods in their own image. The gods of the powerful and comfortable will always approve of and even command the structures of society that favor those in power. The particular, historical, self-serving values of a few become the eternal, unchangeable values of God, who commands that all people obey this social system, which is part of God's eternal plan. In this way, the exploitation and suffering of the oppressed people in a society become sanctioned as the divine will. And where there is belief in life after death, obedient slaves are told they will be rewarded and rebellious ones punished in the afterlife.

We might expect slaves and other exploited people to reject such theology, and they do at times. But remember that those in power control the pulpits, the books, the schools, the churches. And if slaves are caught talking about a god who calls them to be free, you can well imagine how such blasphemy will be punished. Soon the slaves learn to accept the religion of the masters, and to teach it to their children. Should a slave child challenge a god who commands slavery, the parent may well say, "Hush child. The master and God will hear and punish you." To survive, the exploited usually accept the religion of the exploiter—at least in part. Think of how often writers in the New Testament, fearing persecution by the Romans, say "give the enemy no occasion to revile us."

In his letter to the Romans, Paul goes even further:

> [1]Let every person be subject to the governing authorities; for there is no authority except from God, and those authorities that exist have been instituted by God. [2]Therefore whoever resists authority resists what God has appointed, and those who resist will incur judgment. [3]For rulers are not a terror to good conduct, but to bad. Do you wish to have no fear of the authority? Then do what is good, and you will receive its approval, [4]for it is God's servant for your good. But if you do wrong, you should be afraid, for the authority

does not bear the sword in vain! It is the servant of God
to execute wrath on the wrongdoer.

Romans 13:1–4

This passage helped support the medieval doctrine of the
"divine right of kings," and we can well imagine the countless
times it must have been quoted by those in power. The clear
statement seems to be that whatever the political ruler does
must be approved by God, or else God would remove the ruler
from office. The laws created by human beings—however cruel
and exploitive—directly acquire divine support. To rebel
against injustice in the society is to rebel against God.

Religion and society are too complicated for any single
generalization to be adequate. There can be no denying that
religion, including the Christian religion, has often been a
source of moral and social reform, calling people to a vision of
a better world. Prophets have arisen from among the oppressors as well as the oppressed, challenging the status quo and
sounding a call to work for a better world. For such people and
such religious visions we must be grateful.

The clear fact remains, however, that religion, including
Christian religion, has consistently been one of the most effective tools available to the powerful elite for maintaining oppression. Perhaps the most insidious fact is that precisely
because the oppression is believed to be ordained by God, it is
not seen as oppression at all. It surely must be part of God's
just and loving plan (we say) for so many to suffer on behalf of
so few. Loving service, after all, is surely Christlike—especially for slaves! And women. And Third World peoples.

God's Omnipotence as a Central Problem

One crucial feature of traditional Christian theology that
makes it so susceptible to oppressive use, I believe, is its
insistence that God is all powerful. Since God is all-powerful,
Christians have said (or implied) that the world is the way
God wants it to be. Even the misery and injustice of this world
have been seen persistently as part of God's eternal plan.

Generally, the assumption has been that human suffering
is necessary to our spiritual growth. Without it we could not
learn to be loving, sympathetic, or self-sacrificing. One excep-
tionally clear statement of this view comes from the contemporary theologian, John Hick. In his classic study of the prob-

lem of evil, *Evil and the God of Love*, Hick argues at great length that God has intentionally allowed the suffering of this world so that our life can be a process of "soul-making." Soul-making means becoming the kind of loving, caring people capable of eternal communion with God. And this process can only take place in a world filled with suffering, even injustice.

> It seems, then, that in a world that is to be the scene of compassionate love and self-giving for others, suffering must fall upon mankind with something of the haphazardness and inequity that we now experience. It must be apparently unmerited, pointless, and incapable of being morally rationalized. For it is precisely this feature of our common human lot that creates sympathy between man and man and evokes the unselfish kindness and goodwill which are among the highest values of personal life.[3]

The role of suffering in human life is certainly a complex issue. But there can be no mistaking the importance of assuming that God is all-powerful so that whatever happens in the world has been either directly caused or indirectly allowed to happen because of God's infinitely loving wisdom. If the injustice of the world did not finally serve God's purposes, God could, Christians have believed, simply remove it.

Doubtless many readers will object that our traditional images have depicted God as calling us to improve this world, to combat its injustices. That is often true. Such beliefs have led Christians to oppose slavery, unjust laws, exploitive economic systems, and the oppression of sexism. For such theologies we should all be grateful.

But each of these efforts has been undermined by the persistent belief that God is all-powerful. If an all powerful God chooses not to intervene to prevent slavery, to erase poverty, to cleanse the racism and sexism in our hearts, or to end the horrors of war, it must be that these evils play some part in God's plan. And quickly we hear people quoting Romans 13 and 1 Timothy 6 to explain that those in charge really have God's support and approval.

In the following chapters I will explore the ways in which process theology avoids these difficulties and calls us to a better world.

---

[3]John Hick, *Evil and the God of Love* (Macmillan Co., 1966), p. 370f.

CHAPTER 9

A Process Theology of Liberation

Process theology's vision of God directly supports theologies of liberation in three major ways. By affirming the relational character of the Divine as participating in the experience of every creature, process theology offers a picture of a God directly sharing the sufferings of the world. God becomes the victim of injustice and oppression rather than an aloof king. By denying the traditional notion that God is all-powerful, it pulls the props out from under any effort to say that existing social injustices are part of the divine plan. And by focusing on the priority of relational power rather than unilateral power, process theology also builds a natural affinity for the liberation of women by offering better resources for seeing God through feminist categories.

A God Who Suffers and Rejoices with Us

Whitehead referred to God as the "great companion, the fellow sufferer who understands" because the God Whitehead envisioned is one who shares every creature's experience in every moment.

In Elie Wiesel's account of his experiences in the concentration camps, *Night*, he describes the death of a young boy. When hanged, the boy was too light for the rope to do its usual job. Rather than die quickly, he lingered on, gasping for breath, wriggling at the end of the rope, suffocating slowly. One of the prisoners required to watch asked, "Where is God now?" To which another responded, "Here He is—He is hanging here on this gallows...."[1]

Probably that prisoner meant that his faith in God was dying with the boy. Process theists would agree that such suffering rightly proclaims the death of faith in a God who could prevent such suffering but refuses to do so. Appeals to "human agency" cannot mean much to the child on the rope or the prisoners forced to watch.

Process theologians, however, might well have said the same words with a different meaning. "God is at the end of that rope." That is, God is sharing the suffering of the boy, and also the suffering of the prisoners. God also shares the experience of the camp guards and grieves over the destruction of their humanity, of their capacity for human feelings of love and compassion.

This image of God was powerfully expressed by the Rev. Carter Heyward in her sermon on "The Enigmatic God." Heyward struggles with the meaning of the story of Moses receiving the divine name, "I AM." (Or, "I AM WHO I AM," or "I WILL BE WHAT I WILL BE.") Was God being evasive? Perhaps not, Heyward suggests. Perhaps this story forthrightly suggests that God's nature is too dynamic and pervasive to be captured in only one name. God will appear to us in places and ways we never expected, calling us to see the world with a fresh angle of vision. Possibly inspired by Wiesel's story of the hanging, Rev. Heyward challenges us to look for God in unexpected people.

---

[1]Elie Wiesel, *Night* (Bantam Books, 1986), p. 62.

God will hang on the gallows.
God will inspire, fill, overwhelm Handel with
    power and splendor.
God will be battered as a wife, a child, a nigger,
    a faggot.
God will judge with righteousness, justice, mercy
    those who batter, burn, sneer, discriminate,
    or harbor prejudice.
God will have a mastectomy.
God will experience the wonder of giving birth.
God will be handicapped.
God will run the marathon.
God will win.
God will lose.
God will be down and out, suffering, dying.
God will be bursting free, coming to life, for
God will be who God will be.[2]

Heyward's challenge can point us toward another important insight of process theism, that God's justice is not impartiality, but rather omnipartiality. God is not above or beyond or aloof from the interests of the creatures. Rather God shares every point of view, every creature's interests, every joy and every sorrow. But more, God is able to compare each creature's actual experience with what it might have been had we been wiser, kinder, more generous, more compassionate. God not only feels our pain, but adds to it the pain of experiencing the gulf between what is and what might have been. And when the possible joys become actual, when the potential for richness is made real in creatures' lives, God experiences that joy, too.

Such a God can never settle for the inadequate status quo. Such a God can never sanction a state of affairs in which some are victimized, exploited, and oppressed, because God is one of the victims. God can never settle for a world in which we who are in the middle class are merely comfortable, because God knows the awful truth about how much richer and better the world could be for us and others if we lived lives directed and driven by compassion for those who bear the burden of our comfort.

---

[2]Carter Heyward, "The Enigmatic God," *The Witness,* April 1974, p. 5.

A God Who Journeys with Us

Process theology rejects all efforts to identify existing social, political, or economic structures with the eternal will of God. Instead it calls us to see God as struggling to move us toward better, more just structures. The God of process theology is working for liberation in every moment and calls us in every moment to share in the task.

Traditional theologies have always pictured God as totally in control. Even those who affirm "free will" have held that God could reach in at any moment and restrain the devil or a person or touch a human heart with transforming love. Eventually, at the preordained time, Christ will return and usher in the perfect kingdom where all suffering is ended, where all sin is banished, where only love, happiness, and joy remain. Christianity has always held out the very pleasant assurance that the victory is already won, that God is only continuing the miseries of this world for some purpose about which we can only speculate. That there must be a reason why Christ has not returned to banish our pain only seems to prove that (according to traditional theologies) all the injustice and suffering of this world serves some divine purpose.

In process theology there are, frankly, no such guarantees. What is guaranteed is that God is doing everything within divine power to work with us *for* the growth of justice and goodness. The battle is real and ongoing. There are no predetermined outcomes. As so many have come to recognize, *life is a journey*—a process—and it is the quality of the journey with which we must concern ourselves.

Remember, of course, that process theologians do affirm the guarantee that God's love will always be with us along the way, working to make a world in which every creature's journey can be as rich as possible. And beyond this, there is the assurance that whatever happens, God is never ultimately defeated. God will work with whatever is left here and in other parts of the universe. Also, all the values attained during God's adventure with us are preserved eternally in God's life.

Someone might respond to this last paragraph by indignantly retorting: "Well, then, why should God care what happens to us?" The answer is clear. God is the only one who shares fully the pain and loss of all creatures, as well as all our joys. God suffers with us. Furthermore, if we destroy ourselves, there are great values that are lost, which we might have actualized. And finally, of course, God loves us. So naturally God cares what we do to ourselves. But these guarantees are about the nature and love of God, not about what will happen to us.

It might be nice to have guarantees about the future. But they just aren't there. Sometimes people say things like: "Our belief in God's guarantee of victory must be true. Without such a guarantee life would be meaningless." But such outcries are merely complaints, irrelevant to questions of truth. We want guarantees, but what we have is a journey, an adventure, a process—life with all its risks. The God of process theology promises to share that life with us and to work with us for the good of all.

This promise is also a call. The world is not the way God wants it to be. Unjust social structures do *not* reflect God's vision for us. Poverty, hunger, and violence are *not* trials intentionally put into the world by God for our education. They are evils against which God is struggling and against which God calls us to struggle.

Some might complain that a God who lacks the power to part the Red Sea, or overcome the oppressors' thugs, or suddenly give pure hearts to the powerful cannot be a liberating God. It is true that the God of process theism cannot wave a magic wand and end the suffering. Process theology is for those who have given up belief in a picture of God whose only virtue is unused power, or power used selectively for a lucky few. Instead, process theology calls us to accept a world in which we must bear responsibility. God can work in the world; but God can work in our world most effectively, most quickly, through us. On this planet, we are probably the creatures most capable of perceiving and responding to God's vision of a different, better world. God's primary avenue to liberation is through responsive human hearts. We can wait for supernatural miracles or we can roll up our sleeves with God and get to work.

CHAPTER 10

Women's Experience and Process Thought

Whatever we might think about men and women, it is obvious that in Western culture (and most other cultures, too) there are powerful traditions about the differences between the sexes. Many of our traditional images have clearly called men to be independent, unilaterally powerful, rational, dominating, and emotionally stern and aloof. Women have obviously been taught to be dependent upon men (hence the titles Mrs. and Miss, but only Mr.), to be emotional rather than rational, and to be cherishing and nurturing rather than dominating. The classic line, "Wait until your father gets home!" tells us volumes about how we have viewed men and women, and what it means to call God "Father."

It is hardly surprising that many people sensitive to women's issues have seen process theology as an exciting model of God. The view of God as nurturing, cherishing, persuading, participating, and suffering with us seems much closer to traditional feminine values and images than do most traditional pictures of the stern, aloof God. If we use the model of God as Parent, then the process God seems to include the qualities of a mother far more than do traditional models.

Obviously, the real goal is to transcend the temptation to make God appear more like one sex than the other. Nevertheless, we need first to continue the task of hearing, acknowledging, and learning to appreciate the histories, sufferings, values, and insights of those people who have not been in power, whose perspectives have been suppressed in most of the world by the dominant male cultures. With regard to feminism in particular, men and women have far to go in recovering women's history, listening to women's voices, and understanding and appreciating the values women can contribute to our common humanity. As we do this, we must be prepared to let these voices reshape our images of the sacred. Toward that end, I have invited Barbara Hiles Mesle* to contribute her thoughts.

By Barbara

Simply put, feminism seeks the social, economic, and political equality of both sexes. Feminists generally agree that women's culture needs to be recovered and celebrated. Feminists engage with others in seeking a safer, more gentle world for all of creation. These concerns seem to fit very well with those of process thinkers.

But discussions about differences between men and women are like a dry forest, ready to catch fire with the smallest spark. For some very good reasons, both women and men fear generalizations about their nature and behavior. How can we talk about the differences in the ways women and men experience the world without sounding as if there is no affinity— without sounding as if all men think alike and all women think alike? As one of my students put it, "Barbara, if we celebrate uniqueness, don't we just divide people? Don't we perpetuate the stereotypes and differences?"

To put the question differently, since process thinkers and feminists agree that we need to rid our thinking of dualistic

---

*Assistant professor of English, Graceland College.

and hierarchical categories, how can we talk legitimately about "difference"? I would like to explore this topic a bit before connecting feminism and process thought more directly.

Most of us are vividly aware of the ways in which stereotypes are either inadequate or downright false. I remember telling people on my first visit to Europe that I was from Chicago. Invariably they wanted to know if I were rich and a gangster. They seemed relieved, and a tad disappointed, when I assured them I was neither! If we each think of the many groups of which we are members, we can readily identify many ways in which we are different from the other people in those groups.

As Deborah Tannen suggests, "We all know we are unique individuals, but we tend to see others as representative groups. It's a natural tendency, since we must see the world in patterns in order to make sense of it....But this natural and useful ability to see patterns of similarity has unfortunate consequences."[1] These unfortunate consequences are generalizations that offend and mislead us.

At the same time, generalizations can inform and connect us. Common ties leap out at us when we meet someone from our old high school, our hometown, our church, or our family. I agree with Tannen that the "risk of ignoring differences is greater than the danger of naming them. Sweeping something big under the rug doesn't make it go away; it trips you up and sends you sprawling when you venture across the room."[2]

Certainly, many individuals always did exhibit their own personalities irrespective of the accepted "masculine" and "feminine" behavior. Nevertheless, these individuals often paid a price in terms of social acceptance. The familiar playground taunts of "sissy" and "tomboy" are testimony to this price.

Whatever the origin of these complex differences between men and women, patterns do seem to emerge. Many studies have shown that deeply embedded in Western culture, and hence in all of us who live in this culture, is an association of masculinity with competition and femininity with cooperation. This list can be expanded in ways that sound familiar to most of us by now. Just to suggest a few examples, men were/

---

[1] Deborah Tannen, *You Just Don't Understand: Women and Men in Conversation* (William Morrow, 1990), p. 16.

[2] *Ibid.*

are usually expected to be rational problem solvers, concerned for themselves and unconcerned for the feelings of others or even their own feelings. Conversely, women's focus was the affective domain. Since peacekeeping and harmony were its goal, many women were socialized to feel very uncomfortable with conflict or anger and to be self-sacrificing to the extreme. Men's tendency to focus on independence more than intimacy and women's tendency to focus on intimacy more than independence is widely documented and has had negative consequences for our relationships—and for our theology.

Obviously we cannot recognize our cultural obliviousness to the perspectives of women until we listen to women's perspectives. If we ignore all difference, it is easy to impose rigid role distinctions on women and men and to trivialize or malign women's culture. If we ignore all difference, it is easy to expect women to function well within male-dominated structures, but not to expect men to learn female structures. Also, if we artificially assign the "public sphere" to men and the "private sphere" to women, it is easy to miss the talents of individuals whose natural propensities do not match the norm. If we ignore all difference, it is too easy to assume—even unconsciously—that the "male perspective" is the natural and correct one. It is too easy for those who grow up female (or black or homosexual or Jewish or Chicano or...) to suffer the poor self-esteem that comes from assuming that their perceptions are somehow "wrong." The world feminism seeks is a more tolerant one, a world that values diversity at the same time that it affirms the common ties that bind us all together.

This is the same world that process thought seeks. Of course, not all process philosophers think exactly alike any more than all feminists do.[3] But some general claims are possible. Process thought, like feminism, puts relationships at the center of the meaning of our lives. Process thinkers, like feminists, dislike unilateral power and desire to reformulate the whole notion of power so that is is relational—that is, power "with" instead of power "over." Process thought, like feminism, does not treat suffering as an ennobling condition that inevitably leads to growth. Rather, in process theology God suffers with victims. It is the responsibility of the commu-

---

[3] See Sheila G. Davaney, ed., *Feminism and Process Thought* (Edwin Mellen, 1981).

nity to respond with loving support. The goal is to wring good from the pain without ever calling the pain good.

Many thinkers have noted the similarities between the orthodox description of God the Father and the classic stereotypes of desirable male behavior. Men, in this model, were to be rational, controlling, aloof, and authoritative. They needed to be praised and cared for and protected from mundane realities so that they were free to do "important things." The similarities to the orthodox white male God are self-evident. Process thinkers offer a model of God whose key characteristic is love. In this model, intimacy is not feared as antithetical to independence. This God is freed from the burden imposed by being perfectly powerful. God does all God can. God is my advocate and your advocate. God is the advocate of justice for all creatures. With this view of God, meaning is not "out there" somewhere, but "in here" in relationships and in the ordinary and not-so-ordinary colors of our daily lives. But because we are genuinely free and because God cannot over-rule the physical forces of the universe, God cannot control events or guarantee outcomes. This God does not have some mysterious, secret reason for the tragedies in our lives but is working actively with us to create the best that we can be. A peaceful God who is thoroughly relational, a nurturing God who suffers with us, offers a model that would appeal to many feminists.

Process thought's view of freedom is also exciting to a feminist. Since the future genuinely does not exist yet, but rather is constantly being created out of each moment, we are not determined. Our course is not fixed but is flexible. This creates the possibility for genuine hope. We are truly free to take our past and weave from it a new future. We can take the past history of sexism and racism and transform it into a present that is better for ourselves, our children, and all of creation. We can live harmoniously with all of life since everything that lives is holy.

CHAPTER 11

Revelation, Scripture, and Liberation

As part of the doctrine of omnipotence, traditional theologies have usually assumed that God is quite capable of giving clear and unambiguous revelation to whomever God chooses. For this reason, people of all kinds have found it easy to claim to speak for God. This power to speak for God has served directly as one of the most effective religious tools for oppression. If social regulations and customs can claim direct divine origin in the infallible revelations of God, then how can anyone—even the victims—protest? And why should those who benefit feel guilty if their enrichment somehow serves God's greater purposes?

Process theology's approach to revelation destroys any such opportunity to use alleged revelation for purposes of exploitation and oppression.

Christians have always affirmed in one way or another that God is active in their lives, revealing divine love in the world. Yet, a whole range of modern inquiries into the nature and origins of the Bible, Christian doctrines, world religions, and the sociology and psychology of religious consciousness has gradually driven many Christians to the recognition that all that we call revelation—including the scriptures and creeds—expresses the full humanity of its authors. The culture, theology, social and economic setting, and personal biography of the prophet all shape the revelatory experience.

How does process theology speak to these two convictions? The answer, I think, is that process theology embraces both with a breadth and depth that must challenge us to rethink the whole notion of revelation. What if we took with full seriousness the concept that divine revelation is as universal as divine love? What if we finally accepted, without exception, the interweaving of the divine and human in the whole world?

Revelation as Continuing, Universal, and Interwoven with the World

According to process theology, God is revealed to every creature in every moment in every place in the universe. God does not single out a select few prophets to talk to while excluding the billions of others. God's self-revelation is the ground of every person's freedom. God's self-revelation of love comes to all people in every moment of their lives, calling *every* person toward a vision of truth, beauty, and goodness.

This does not mean, of course, that all people are equal in insight, sensitivity, intelligence, and responsiveness to the divine.

There surely are people with greater love, broader vision, and greater foresight. There are people with greater relational power to feel the sufferings of the oppressed, agonize over the injustice they see, and call us to transform our world. There are people who, in varying degrees, are able to push beyond their cultural conditioning. In short, there are prophetic people. But this is a fact about the world, not about the divine plan. God calls us all to be prophetic, but we are not all equally able or willing to see.

At the same time that it affirms that God's self-revelation is universal, process theology clearly accounts for the fact that all of us, including our most prophetic giants, see God "through a glass, darkly." That glass is the influence of the world around us. We do experience God, say process theologians, but our experience of God is one of many threads that we weave together. God's unique power in the world is to be eternal, universal, and infinitely patient. God is always there, while voices in the world come and go. But the world's voices have the advantage of being louder, more coercive, and—alas—often more attractive to us given our selfishness and insecurity.

There are many voices in the world calling us toward good things. But while God always calls us to love, the world all too often calls us to selfish love. While God may call us to risk for love, the world often calls us to play it safe. While God calls us to a long range vision of a better world, the present world often calls us to sacrifice the future for present desires and fears.

Tragically, we easily mistake our own desires for God's call. We distort God's vision by forcing it to conform to our own selfish plans. One especially sad instance, mentioned previously, is the way in which the example of Christ's sacrificial love was manipulated by many Christians (including some New Testament authors) to keep Christian slaves in line. The same strategy has helped to keep women in line.

> [1]Wives, in the same way, accept the authority of your husbands....[5]It was in this way long ago that the holy women who hoped in God used to adorn themselves by accepting the authority of their husbands. [6]Thus Sarah obeyed Abraham and called him Lord.
>
> 1 Peter 3:1, 5–6

When the Israelites were wandering in the wilderness, looking for a land of their own, they easily believed that Yahweh was offering them exclusive rights to the land of Canaan. That translated into a divine call to slaughter and enslave the current inhabitants. Consider Deuteronomy 20:10f (JB) presented in the Bible as the very words of Yahweh.

> [10]When you advance to the attack on any town, first offer it terms of peace. [11]If it accepts these and opens its gates to you, all the people to be found in it shall do forced labour for you and be subject to you. [12]But if it

refuses peace and offers resistance, you must lay siege to it. ¹³Yahweh your God shall deliver it into you power and you are to put all its menfolk to the sword. ¹⁴But the women, the children, the livestock and all that the town contains, all its spoil, you may take for yourselves as booty. You will devour the spoil of your enemies which Yahweh your God has delivered to you.

¹⁵That is how you will treat the far-distant towns not belonging to the nations near you. ¹⁶But as regards the towns of those peoples which Yahweh your God gives you as your own inheritance, you must not spare the life of any living thing. ¹⁷Instead, you must lay them under ban, the Hittites, Amorites, Cannanites, Perizzites, Hivites and Jebusites, as Yahweh your God commanded, ¹⁸so that they may not teach you to practise all the detestable practices they have in honour of their gods and so cause you to sin against Yahweh your God.

How sad that their vision of a divine call to liberation from Egyptian slavery should be transformed into a cry to enslave and slaughter other innocent people in the name of "the promised land" and religious purity.

Conversely, however, we can see that even among the biblical justifications for slavery and sexism there were moments of greater insight pointing toward a greater liberation. Rather than trying to justify the human shortsightedness of biblical people, we can acknowledge it, while still seeing them as sharing with us in the same long struggle for a greater vision of liberation.

Imagine the God of process theology as one who continually calls for a vision of liberation, for a vision of universal human dignity and equality. Each person hears that. But each person hears that within a cultural context that distorts and narrows that vision. Consider as an example Leviticus 25:1, 39–43 (RSV).

The LORD said to Moses on Mount Sinai.... ³⁹"And if your brother becomes poor beside you, and sells himself to you, you shall not make him serve as a slave: ⁴⁰he shall be with you as a hired servant and a sojourner.... ⁴²For they are my servants, whom I brought forth out of the land of Egypt; they shall not be sold as slaves."

There is a powerful principle of liberation at work here: "We have experienced slavery and know how wrong it is. God's way is a way of liberation, not of bondage."

[6]Is not this the sort of fast that pleases me
—it is the Lord Yahweh who speaks—
to break unjust fetters
and undo the thongs of the yoke,

to let the oppressed go free,
and break every yoke,
[7]to share your bread with the hungry,
and shelter the homeless poor,

to clothe the man you see to be naked
and not turn from your own kin?
[8]Then will your light shine like the dawn
and your wound be quickly healed over.

Your integrity will go before you
and the glory of Yahweh behind you.
[9]Cry, and Yahweh will answer;
call, and he will say, 'I am here.'
Isaiah 58:6–9a (JB)

The biblical authors, alas, were not often able to see this principle as applying beyond the Hebrew community (see Leviticus 25:44–46), but such insights can have a cumulative effect over time. Later Jewish thinkers, of course, extended this insight into a universal principle. And eventually, as the message of Jesus moved into the larger Gentile world, New Testament writers could see that it was not only Jews who were servants of God, and hence called to liberation. Paul was able to see, at least briefly, that this vision extends even further.

There is no longer Jew or Greek, there is no longer slave or free, there is no longer male and female; for all of you are one in Christ Jesus.
Galatians 3:28

Unfortunately, of course, Christians have rarely been able to extend this principle beyond the boundaries of Christianity.

So imagine, again, God reaching out to the biblical peoples, saying, "Respect all creatures. Love all creatures. Liberate all creatures. Treat all creatures with dignity." But given their social and historical context, this cry was heard only occasionally and dimly as, "Maybe we shouldn't enslave other Israelites"; "Maybe even slaves deserve some protection"; and "Maybe even women deserve just a little respect." We, of course, are only beginning to see further than they did (and sometimes not as far).

In traditional theology, based on the assumption that God can reveal God's will clearly, directly, and fully, and has done so to the prophets, the limited insights of a few people in one culture become regarded as God's final word. The results have been tragic for slaves, women, homosexuals, and people from different religions. The authority of the Bible has been a major source of the justification for each form of oppression.

In process theology we are able to see that their limited vision is not the revelation. Rather, God's struggle to break through the world's barriers, to reveal the divine vision through the dark glass, is an ongoing struggle that included them, but includes us as well, and those who will follow us.

Process theologians see God as revealing to us the same call, the same vision of universal dignity. In our day, after centuries of struggle, we seem to be able to hear it more clearly with regard to overt slavery, though we are far from seeing the vision of a world without exploitation and oppression. We are beginning to see the vision of the dignity of women, though that struggle, too, has far to go. We have barely begun to hear the call to respect homosexual persons, to envision universal human community, or to respect the rights of animals.

Process theologians see revelation as an ongoing process of divine call and human response. There are moments of greater insight by people who articulate that vision to us with greater clarity than most. But those moments and those people are always within a historical context. We must never think of revelation as final and complete, but always as continuing.

CHAPTER 12

Committed Relativism: An Approach to Ethics and Global Community

Torturing a person to death or slaughtering them in the name of Jesus Christ, who called us to love our neighbors and even our enemies, seems incredible to us. Yet, we know that it has been a common event in Christian history. And even more sadly, such values are still defended. A recent article in *Ministry* magazine defended the biblical claim that God had commanded the Israelites to practice genocide against the Canaanites (as mentioned in chapter 11 here).[1] Given the author's belief in a literal hell, and his belief in the Canaanites' "irremediable wickedness," "God's authorization of their total

---

[1]Tim Crosby, "Does God Get Angry?" *Ministry: International Journal for Clergy* (July 1990), 8–11 (Seventh Day Adventist, 12501 Old Columbia Pike, Silver Spring, MD 20904).

destruction is justified, even merciful..." (p. 10). Better to slaughter babies now than let them produce more babies who will also burn in hell.

Personally, I don't want to be around people who are so rigidly sure of their religious and moral infallibility that they can approve of slaughtering innocent children in the name of love. Especially, I want such people to stay far away from my children. Dogmatism is dangerous.

I am also frightened, however, by those people who, in reaction to such violence-embracing dogmatism, proclaim a total relativism in which every belief and every value is just as good as every other. If they really believe that, then they have no grounds for objecting to the beliefs and values of the dogmatists who approve of genocide!

People who think carefully about ethics often feel torn between the opposed dangers of dogmatism and total relativism. If we claim that there is a solid, eternal foundation for declaring what is right and wrong, then we risk becoming so dogmatic that, like the Spanish Inquisition, we justify torturing people to force them to accept our religion or ethics. But if, to escape that evil, we embrace total relativism and say that everyone can do whatever they want, then we have no basis for objecting to torture. Our common sense tells us there must be a middle ground, but it needs clear expression.

The differences between cultures intensify the difficulty of this challenge. People have long recognized that what is considered a grave sin punishable under the law of one culture may be perfectly acceptable, even commendable, in another. And what one religion holds as sacred truth seems blasphemous to another. These facts lead many people directly to radical relativism, to the denial of any grounds for criticizing another culture or religion, and ultimately to the denial of any grounds for criticizing anything as immoral. This is what I call total or radical relativism. Within radical relativism we might dislike the concentration camps, but we could claim no grounds for declaring them immoral.

While these difficulties relate directly to our daily efforts to get along with each other (given our individual differences about what is right and wrong) the urgent quest for global community—driven by threats of global pollution, overpopulation, and nuclear annihilation—gives new importance to the search for some middle ground between dogmatism and radical relativism. How can we live together in one world without approving of culturally based oppressions like sexism, racism, and caste systems? What kind of ethical framework will best help us cooperate in building liberating societies of justice and peace? And what kind of religion can support such an ethic?

Committed Relativism

"Committed relativism" is my name for the conviction that it is possible to make legitimate value judgments within and between different lifestyles, cultures, and religions without claiming that there is only one absolute right and wrong, only one absolutely best action, lifestyle, culture, or religion. Committed relativism is the insistence that some actions are immoral, that some lifestyles are unhealthy, and that some cultures are self-destructive, while still positively insisting that there are many different actions, lifestyles, cultures, and religions that create and perpetuate rich values.

Committed relativism is challenging in that it requires us to be open-minded without being empty-minded. It requires us to listen and learn from others, but not simply to accept or approve whatever they say. There are no absolute guidelines by which I can say that one culture is right and another wrong, but I don't have to approve of Nazism or the KKK. I can even fight against the Nazi culture without claiming that American individualism is superior, say, to Japanese community-oriented identity. And, I can recognize that what may be loving in an American culture—hugging someone at the airport—might be embarrassing and unkind within Japanese culture.

There are reasons why process thinkers are naturally led to a committed relativism. Basically, this has to do with the focus on reality as constituted by experience and relationships. Reflecting on the ways in which, in each moment, we must bring into some kind of order a wide and often conflicting range of relationships and values has led most process thinkers to reflect on the category of beauty. Beauty involves both harmony and contrast. Too much harmony means monotony and triviality in experience. Too much contrast leads to destructive discord. Yet we learn in life that even a very healthy balance in our ideas, occupations, and relationships can sometimes grow stale so that for the sake of continued growth we must pursue novelty and adventure on the borders of chaos. Life is a continual balancing between stability and novelty, harmony and discord. Life is a continual process of creating order in our experience. "Beauty" is the category that process thinkers often use to discuss this basic reality.

You don't have to be a process philosopher to share the ethic of committed relativism. For that reason I will settle for this brief explanation and focus on the practical implications. Let me only say that while you don't have to be a process thinker to be a committed relativist, it can help.

The Plurality of Values

Inspired by reflection on the concept of beauty, process thinkers reject the idea that there is only one form of goodness (except perhaps in highly abstract terms). As an example, consider the idea of someone writing a symphony so beautiful that the whole world would say: "That is perfect! Now we need no more symphonies." Or a painting so perfect that we need no more paintings. Absurd! How much more absurd to suggest that a symphony could be so perfect that we would no longer find value in paintings or poetry.

Beauty comes in many forms. It is inherently impossible for one symphony to express all the possible forms of beautiful music, paintings, or sculpture. It is especially absurd when we consider that human beings (and probably other creatures, too) feel some drive toward novelty and adventure. No matter how wonderful one symphony is, we need variety and novelty to satisfy our sense of beauty. While we like the security and richness that come with the familiar, mere repetition like the proverbial water torture is not merely boring, but positively destructive. The thought of an accident or disease reducing a person to a "human vegetable" is one of our deepest fears. We need variety and novelty for richness of life. Our enjoyment of Beethoven's fifth symphony is actually enriched by the experience of listening to other kinds of music at other times.

Beauty, Life, and Committed Relativism

Just as there is no one right way to create beauty, there is no single right way for a person to live. We might abstractly say, "Have a rich and loving life!" But there are many ways to live richly and lovingly. Indeed, we positively need people to live in different ways. We would not want everyone to become a physician or a carpenter or a farmer. We need and are enriched by the diversity of human life. It is absurd to suggest that all that is good about life is captured in one career or one way of expressing love. Translating the abstract commandment "Love!" into concrete actions demands a world of novelty, creativity, diversity, and adventure.

What is crucial to recognize is that this need for diversity, for different ways of living, is not a denial of all values. It is not radical relativism.

Perhaps this point can be better illustrated through the culinary arts and nutrition. Some edible things in this world are poisonous, and many nonpoisonous foods may be terribly unhealthy for a few, or many, or all people—as we learn every day. Also, nutritionists are constantly learning about what our bodies need in terms of vitamins and other nutrients. So while the needs of one person may vary somewhat from those of another, we fully accept the idea that some foods are much healthier than others, and that some are downright deadly.

Fortunately, even once we screen out what is unhealthy, there is a wide variety of foods, in myriad combinations, capable of keeping us healthy. Foods differ from culture to culture, region to region, and family to family. There isn't just one right meal to serve. Indeed, we would quickly tire of even our favorite food if there were no variety. But the main point is this. We practice a kind of committed relativism toward foods all the time. We accept a wide range of culinary tastes and values without pretending that all edibles are equally good for our bodies.

The same is true of careers and lifestyles. We can affirm with all our might that being a competent, caring physician is better than being a professional assassin, without insisting that everyone be a physician. Alongside this is the recognition that actions that are morally and otherwise better for a physician may not be so for a carpenter. A medically untrained carpenter would rarely be justified in sticking a scalpel into a person. And what may be a loving and moral act within one culture might possibly be unloving and immoral within another. If I meet my wife at the airport I will surely give her a big hug to show my love. But it usually would be very insensitive and unloving if I were to greet a Japanese friend in this manner in Japan.

So, just as there is no perfect symphony and no perfect menu, there is no perfect way to live. Speaking concretely, the idea of a perfect life makes no more sense than a perfect painting. Yet, we can recognize that some ways of living are far more likely to help people live rich lives. Beating and molesting children closes down rather than opens up their abilities to sustain a wide range of intimate human relationships, and such relationships are usually the most crucial components in happy living.

Global Community and Relational Power

As the world grows smaller with improved communications and faster travel, the challenge of pluralistic living becomes more vital. Ordinary individuals who cannot tolerate people with other ways of living do not usually have access to nuclear weapons. But when nations of people suspicious of each other are forced into closer and closer contact, the result can be disastrous if each works from a value system that affirms its own normality as ultimate morality.

Here we must return to the theme of relational power. Relational power is the ability to be responsive to a wide range of relationships—of ideas, values, feelings, people, etc.—to create ourselves out of these diverse relationships, and to affect others by having first been affected by them. In education this obviously means the ability to learn, to take in new information and new perspectives, to creatively shape our own ideas and beliefs out of them, and to communicate to others in ways responsive to what we have learned from them. In human relationships relational power means the ability to feel the values and feelings of others—their hopes, fears, joys, sorrows, loves, and suspicions—to create our own lives and values in response to them, and then to relate back to them in ways that show that we have taken them creatively into our own life first.

Other people become a part of us. The question is whether we will embrace or resist that reality. Traditionally we have contrasted love (being sensitive and caring) with power (the ability to stand aloof and unilaterally affect others without being affected by them). In the relational model of power true power is shown through love. Of course relational power is more effective if we want to help other people live richer, fuller, more loving lives. Unilateral power is more effective if we are interested in dominating, oppressing, controlling, and destroying people. Our values will determine the kind of power we want to nurture.

In the long run, however, unilateral power is self-defeating for any person who wants their own life to be loving, full, and rich in relationships. When we impoverish, oppress, dominate, and destroy others, we cannot enjoy loving relationships with them, and thus we impoverish both ourselves and them.

The power of Jesus lay precisely in his ability to sustain loving relationships with those who were supposed to be his enemies. Sinners and Roman tax collectors, Roman soldiers, and the others who rejected him were not rejected by him. He continued to create himself in response to them in ways they could not defeat. They could not make him stop loving them. He could sustain the loving relationship despite their relational weakness (hidden behind their unilateral power).

If we are to nurture the capacity of people to live in a global community (or, indeed, in any community), we must nurture their relational power. We must learn ourselves, and help others learn, the value of being open to new values, new lifestyles, and new cultures so that they enrich us rather than frightening us. Concretely, this begins by raising children lovingly, and continues in their daily education. We must model for them openness and care, excitement over other ideas, other languages, other styles of dress and food, and mainly other people.

Seeing people who are different as wonderful resources for mutually enriching relationships is the key to global community. That is what committed relativism, the process sense of beauty, and the emotional strength of relational power are all about. With these approaches to human differences in values and religion we will be less likely to slaughter innocent children "for their own good." You don't have to be a process thinker to appreciate these insights, but it helps.

CHAPTER 13

Religious Pluralism

One of the vital and challenging global issues facing us today is the diversity of world religions. Obviously the ideas of committed relativism, beauty in relationships, and relational power all apply here as much as in any other area. But the religious issue is complicated in special ways. How should committed Christians account for the existence of these religions if the Christian God is truly loving and universally self-revealing? Why hasn't Christ spoken to them as well? Or, if Christ has, why haven't they responded? And how shall we relate to those people in a manner that respects their integrity while expressing our desire to share the gospel Christians have received? To set the stage for process theology's response to these questions we need to remind ourselves of how sadly Christianity has dealt with them in the past.

A Sad History

For centuries most Christians lived with virtually no contact with or even knowlege of people in other religions. Christians have always known, of course, about Jews, and have usually viewed them as Christ killers, infidels, and people condemned to eternal hellfire. At best Jews were tolerated and treated as inferiors; at worst they were regularly brutalized, raped, and slaughtered by their Christian neighbors. Christian attitudes toward people in Eastern religions were essentially the same, though until recently geographical separation prevented most direct conflicts other than the crusades. The war that rages in Iraq as I write underscores the need for us to improve understanding between the world's religious communities.

Destructive Christian attitudes toward other world religions (as well as hostilities between Christian denominations) have resulted partly from ordinary human prejudices toward people who are different. But these problems also have theological foundations. We have assumed, in line with the attitudes of biblical writers, that the truth of our religion is perfectly clear to all people, so that those who reject it do so out of a perverse self-deception. A prime example of such theology can be found in Paul's letter to the Romans:

> [18]For the wrath of God is revealed from heaven against all ungodliness and wickedness of men who by their wickedness suppress the truth. [19]For what can be known about God is plain to them, because God has shown it to them. [20]Ever since the creation of the world his invisible nature, namely, his eternal power and deity, has been clearly perceived in the things that have been made. So they are without excuse; [21]for although they knew God they did not honor him as God....[25]they exchanged the truth about God for a lie.
>
> 1:18–21, 25 (RSV)

The propensity to view all people with other religious beliefs as intellectually dishonest and/or spiritually lazy or perverse arises, as do many problems we have examined, from the traditional assumption that God is all-powerful. Such a God has no difficulty in providing people with plain and unambiguous revelations of the truth. When people who believe they have received such revelations are asked why others have not, they must logically respond either that those people were not faithful enough to receive the revelation, or that they did receive it but faithlessly rejected it, exchanging the truth about God for a lie.

As the passage from Romans suggests, the scriptural support for such a stance is strong, as illustrated in the letters of John in the New Testament. Despite "John's" beautiful words of love, those Christians who disagree with the author are consistently condemned as liars, deceivers, and antichrists. In one case, (2 John 10–11) the Johannine author even directs his followers to refuse to greet the dissenters or to welcome them into their houses. So much for interfaith dialogue (as shown in 3 John 9–10).

A Process View

Thankfully, many Christians know better than to be so provincial or closed-minded. We know from daily experience in our pluralistic societies that the world is filled with people who disagree with us on theological and other issues but who are still fine and loving people. The question that still confronts us is how we can account for religious diversity given the Christian conviction that God loves all people and reveals the divine love and will to each of them.

Process theology has a straightforward answer that we have already seen applied to our understanding of scripture. It is simply not within God's power to unilaterally span the gulf between us. We always, necessarily, experience God from within the context of our own world. That world is shaped by our historical setting, our culture, our finances, our social status, our sex, our past decisions, our intelligence, and all of the rest of our personal biography. God's revelation to us is continually interwoven with the influence of all the other entities forming the web of relationships out of which we create ourselves. We never encounter God in a vacuum.

If we take seriously the power of history and culture, we should hardly be surprised that people in India in 500 B.C. experienced God, and were worked with by God, differently than were people in Palestine at the time of Jesus, or middle-class Americans today. God loves and calls all of them, but they experience that love and call differently. And, indeed, God surely addresses that love in forms appropriate to their circumstances and calls them to actions appropriate to their personal and cultural situations. What is loving and constructive in one culture may not be so in another.

Perhaps I should pause to distinguish this view from another that might sound very similar. It is common for people to explain difficult passages of scripture by saying that God was just speaking to those people in terms they could understand. For example, the authors of the Bible assumed that the world was flat, covered by a hard dome and surrounded by water. They also thought that God had given them the "promised land" and so had both commanded and enabled the Israelites to slaughter and enslave the Canaanites who already lived there. When we assume that God is omnipotent and able to reveal whatever God wishes, then the idea that God really said these things as a way of working with those people creates a terrible picture of God. Why would God, for example, tell people, "Thou shalt not kill," and then command them to conduct mass slaughter on the grounds that genocide was the best they could understand?

Process theology is saying something very different. On the one hand, process theology rejects such simple notions of plenary, verbal revelation, so we never see scripture as the words of God. They are always the words of human beings struggling to express their encounters with the Divine—encounters always filter through their conditioned humanity. On the other hand, process theologians are suggesting that God will really work in different ways with different people. This is only to say that God's love is both responsive and creative. God continually responds to the actual situations of the world to call people toward the good. And God's love is creative because there are many different ways in which God can create good in the world. So there is a combination of people perceiving God differently because of their different cultural experiences, and of God responding by working in different ways with people in different cultures.

Beauty, Committed Relativism, and Religious Pluralism

The issues discussed in the last chapter apply here quite directly. There are many good ways in which people can live, and those ways may not be entirely compatible. It may be entirely possible that there are values to be experienced with a Buddhist, Muslim, or Hindu way of life that cannot be fully enjoyed within a Christian context. And these values may be just as good as those values Christians enjoy—just different. We may also discover that we can, to some extent, learn from each other ways of combining our religous insights to capture new and even richer values that we might not have been able to discover if the world had been entirely Christian or entirely Buddhist. In that case, the world as a whole is richer for the very fact of religious diversity. The different world religions (and even different Christian denominations) appear in this case not as a theological problem but as a resource.

Consider the example of Buddhism. Buddhism is rooted deeply in the fundamental fact that human experience involves suffering. This is the first principle of the Buddha's Four Noble Truths. Let me paraphrase a story that could be of great value in a dialogue between Christian and Buddhist thought. According to this story a man came to the Buddha and said, in effect: "If you will explain to me the truths about whether the world is eternal or not eternal, whether God exists or does not exist and other such truths, I will become your disciple." But the Buddha replied that he would not waste time explaining the nature of eternity, God, or other such truths since they had nothing to do with religion. For religion has to do with suffering and our escape from suffering, and that is the problem about which the Buddha would teach.

Christians could profit from dialogue with such a perspective. How often have we bemoaned our tendencies to become so caught up in defending our theological doctrines that we not only neglect human beings, but actually torture and slaughter each other to defend our beliefs? Couldn't we be enriched by learning from the Buddha about the proper place of theology in human life? At the same time, I believe that Christians have something important to share with Buddhists about the positive values of joy in life.

In other words, I am suggesting that from the perspective of process theology there can be more religious *beauty*—more mutually enriching values—in a world with religious diversity than in a world without it. We can learn to celebrate the very existence and values of other world religions as a gift from God.

Committed relativism in this context provides a healthy framework for interfaith dialogue. It allows people to affirm the value of their own tradition while positively affirming that other traditions can also offer creative values. Both of these elements are crucial if there is to be genuine dialogue and not merely taking turns at attempts to convert each other.

Issues of Religious Truth

So far we have discussed committed relativism primarily in terms of values, but it also applies to issues of truth. In this arena committed relativism is essentially the same approach to the search for truth that has long characterized the best of philosophy and science. We commit ourselves to the best that we know now, to the beliefs that are most strongly supported by our experience, our testing, and our careful thinking. We commit ourselves to these beliefs just to the extent that they are supported by the evidence: neither more nor less. But we recognize that even the most powerfully supported of our beliefs must ultimately be open to reconsideration if new evidence or new ideas suggest better insights into the truth we seek. Persons engaged in religious dialogue must surely carry this ethic of philosophical openness, mutual respect, and committed relativism into the discussion.

For example, people affirming process theology's account of religious diversity are claiming, in some degree, to give a truer account than some others. This may seem to be provincial and self-defeating, but I don't think it is. To offer a perspective on a problem is not inherently to offer it dogmatically. It is perfectly possible to have a good idea and to defend it while still listening respectfully and thoughtfully to the ideas of others. And process theologians are not necessarily claiming that their particular conception of the divine reality precludes the truth of many insights of other traditions. Not all ideas can be true—some do exclude others. But many truths are more compatible than might first appear.

The crucial issue for Christians, of course, is the divinity of Jesus. Can that be true and still leave room for the truth of non-Christian religions? That will be the topic of the next chapter.

CHAPTER 14

Jesus

A crucial example of the way truths may be more compatible than we think is suggested by the process theologians' understanding of Jesus as the Christ. (There are, of course, diverse views among process thinkers on this topic. But there is also much common ground on which I shall try to tread.) It is, I think, a particular virtue of process theology that it is able to treat Jesus in a way respectful of both the Christian tradition and the truth of other religious traditions.

Problems

The traditional views of Jesus form the greatest barrier to Christian dialogue with other religions. If Jesus was the one and only true incarnation of God, and if we can be saved into heaven only by belief in that doctrine, then people in all other religions are hopelessly lost. In contrast, religions like Hinduism and Bahai' are much more tolerant, allowing that divinity may enter the world in many people in many times. Given the Christian claim that God's love is universal, the approaches of these other religions sometimes seem to express Christian values more fully than does Christianity itself.

Christians have also been plagued by the problem of why God had to go to all this trouble to have the incarnation. In order to have a savior, God first had to assure that there would be a fall from which to save us: no fall, no savior. And then God had to predestine poor Judas to betray Jesus. And Jesus had to die or else it would all be a failure. Strangest of all, if people *had* responded to Jesus's message and *not* crucified him, if everyone had become loving and peaceful, it seems the whole plan of salvation would have collapsed. If Jesus the preacher and teacher had succeeded, Christ the Savior would have failed. A paradox, to say the least.

The logical problems with traditional approaches to the incarnation itself are also obvious and well known. Everyone admits that calling Jesus both fully human and fully divine has meant embracing blatant contradictions. Belief in these contradictions has simply been seen as a test of faith. If we were to look back at the history of the development of these ideas we could appreciate sympathetically the struggle of early Christians to affirm both that Jesus really shared our human struggles and that they had somehow encountered divinity through him. But however much we may appreciate these struggles, many Christians today simply have no interest in testing faithfulness by believing contradictions.

The problem rests partly in the assumption that a human soul is some kind of "thing" (perhaps a substance) that first exists and then enters into relationships with other "things." John Cobb, Jr., observed that in traditional "substance" theologies the problem of the incarnation is made insoluble at the outset because "divine" and "human" are viewed as mutually exclusive substances. Jesus is said to be of both divine substance and human substance, yet these are defined as opposites. It would be like trying to push two solid objects into the same space. To make room for more of one you have to carve out some of the other. In the same way, the traditional categories have meant that for Jesus to be more fully divine the human part had to be pushed out. Hence the impossible contradiction, the logical absurdity, of affirming Jesus as fully human and fully divine.

Incarnation: A Process Alternative

Rather than thinking of the world in terms of substances, consider the implications of the process view that the world is composed of drops of experienced relationships. Neither God nor a human soul first exists and then happens to have relationships with others. Each human soul arises out of a set of social (including biological) relationships from which it creates itself. Those relationships—those people and events—out of which we create ourselves are literally part of us.

Since a human soul is a process, not a substance, "fully human" is not a closed category. In one sense, we can and should define *human* so as to protect the rights of the weakest among us and to assure that people who are different are not treated as subhuman. But in another context we all recognize that there is no specific limit to how much we enter into those kinds of relationships that are what humanity is all about. In this sense, we become more fully human as we become more loving, more fully related to others, more responsive to our environment, etc.

We might say that Jesus was responsive to God in a special way, that Jesus chose to respond fully to God's call. Yet, this way of putting the matter fails to express fully the process-relational vision that we are continually creating ourselves out of our social relationships. The "other" becomes part of the "self." So when we say we are experiencing God's call and responding to it, we are actually, in the process-relational vision, taking God into ourselves and creating ourselves out of God. God becomes incarnate in our lives. So the ethical affirmation that Jesus responded fully to God's call is transformed into a theological affirmation that Jesus incarnated the divine Word in human form.

This incarnation act, however, was not settled in a single event. Rather, Jesus had to continue to decide to incarnate the divine Word in his life. But this process was cumulative. Having made the preliminary choices, Jesus began a process by which each new "Yes" to God brought Jesus more fully into unity with the Divine Logos. Each moment of his life became "co-constituted" by a life fully shaped by God's call in the past, and by full responsiveness to God's call in the new present. Jesus, unlike other people, was able to draw on past decisions that had fully lived out God's call to him. That enabled God to call him to possibilities that would otherwise have been impossible. Possibilities opened up for Jesus that do not open up for the rest of us because we have not made the earlier decisions to prepare for them.

Cobb suggests that Jesus became able to incarnate the Divine Logos in his life. In doing so Jesus became more loving, more sensitive, more responsive, more relationally powerful. This made Jesus both more fully human and more fully divine. For in a relational theology there is no contradiction between Jesus incarnating both humanity and divinity in this way. To be more loving is to be *both* more fully human *and* more fully divine. To be more relationally powerful, more capable of sharing the sufferings of others with healing love, is to be *both* more human *and* more divine.

In ways very responsive to the Christian tradition, Cobb uses the symbol *Christ* for that eternal call of God to the world, that eternal lure for goodness, truthfulness, and beauty. This call is indeed a dimension of the divine life, not something separate from or accidental to divinity. Our experience of God's lure is an experience of the divine being. So the incarnation of God's eternal call is an incarnation of the divine life in the finite world. Hence, Cobb says to us, Jesus became the Christ, the incarnation of the divine call in the world.

The Fall: A Process Alternative

Process theology also avoids the whole, strange business of God needing for humans to fall, for Judas to betray Jesus, for Jesus to fail to convince people, and for the people to crucify Jesus in order for Jesus to save us.

Like many contemporary Christians, process theologians recognize the Genesis story of the fall as a mythical expression of the human condition rather than as a literal event. Our falling short is an ongoing fact about our lives, not about one moment in our past. We may be "fallen," but there is no "fall"; there is only the ongoing process by which God continually works creatively in the world.

As human beings gradually evolved in the world and became capable of moral and religious sensitivity, they also became capable of hatred and cruelty. That is, our ancestors developed into creatures with greater capacity both to accept and reject God's call. At one point in human history, a person named Jesus responded to God's call with amazing fullness. If the world around him had responded too, or had responded to the incarnation of God's love among them, then the world could be transformed and people could experience God and each other in ways they never had before. Sadly, the world chose not to do so very fully. Some did respond in part, and hence the Christian religion was born. Something good happened, but God surely hoped for more, and always hopes for more.

Why, then, did Jesus suffer and die on the cross? Because God could not prevent it.[1] God called others, too; not just Jesus. Indeed, God called (and always calls) all people. We can imagine Jesus responding to that call by taking three steps forward while most people take two steps back. Consequently, it was precisely by responding to God's call, by incarnating divine love in the world, that Jesus made other people see the unlovingness of their own lives and their own failure to respond. Not surprisingly, many people resented Jesus for this revelation of their sinfulness and killed him for it. Having called Jesus into love, God could not then rescue him.

It was not necessary for Jesus to die as part of some eternal plan predestined by God from all eternity. Jesus probably—and God surely—foresaw cruel death as a possibility if he unshakably pursued his course. Still, Jesus became the kind of person who could not really choose to turn away from the path of love even if that path meant death. He and God, we may assume, hoped all along that people would respond with love rather than hate, but most did not. And so Jesus, through his relational power of love, turned even their hatred into a kind of victory. Jesus and God redeemed from this sad event the good that could be gotten. It would have been better if everyone had responded by becoming like Jesus. But since everyone did not, God and Jesus creatively drew from the

---

[1]I am indebted for these ideas to the Rev. Bernard Lee, S.M., in his excellent article, "The Helplessness of God," *Encounter*, Vol. 38:4 (Autumn, 1977), pp. 325–336.

tragedy the best they could, working to prepare the way for God's continuing call to us all. So successful has this redemptive process been that Christians have come to view the cross of Christ as God's greatest victory, and as the paradigm of how good can be redeemed from suffering.

Christ and Religious Pluralism

This view of Jesus as the incarnation of the Christ is obviously shaped by much of the Christian tradition, while at the same time reshaping that tradition in important ways. One of the most vital ways in which the process view of Jesus is responsive to new understandings is the way in which it opens the way for interreligious dialogue. Perceiving Jesus as incarnating the divine lure for him does not preclude seeing other people as incarnating the divine lure in other times and places.

Every person incarnates the divine call—i.e., incarnates God!—to some degree. Process theology opens the door to perceiving people like the Buddha or Gandhi as powerful incarnators of the Logos within their own cultural frameworks. And for reasons explained in the previous chapter, it is entirely possible that what God called the Buddha to do in his culture may have been different in some ways from the call to Jesus in his cultural setting, or to Gandhi in his. God's call is always toward richer, fuller, more loving life for people, but there isn't just one way to live lovingly or richly. So given their different cultural settings we might well expect God to call Jesus and Buddha and Gandhi in somewhat different ways. We should not be surprised, in this worldview, to see both points of strong similarity, as in a call for compassion toward others, and points of significant difference in the messages of those who are called in different cultures.

The challenge of religious pluralism is an important dimension of the contemporary quest for justice, peace, and human liberation. As modern technologies of travel and communication bring us more nearly into a single global community, it will be increasingly vital that we develop understandings of religion that enable us to treat each other with respect, without losing sight of the values our own tradition has preserved. I believe that process theology has much to offer in this quest.

CHAPTER 15

Prayer, Liberation, and Healing

Prayer is an act of worship. The primary purpose of worship is to center our lives around that which we perceive as sacred.

The way we usually pray is really very curious. Our prayers rarely fit our vision of God. I don't want to suggest for a moment that prayers need to pass some theological test before they can be powerful moments of worship. We all know how often we struggle for words—and with words—and are not quite sure how to capture and express what is in our hearts. Especially in moments of stress, but also in everyday events, none of us would want people following us around checking to see if our prayers precisely matched our theologies.

All the same, if we take prayer seriously, it makes sense to pause from time to time and think about why and how we do it.

Since what we say can shape what we feel and do, it pays to give some attention to our words. Consider some examples.

Dear God, we ask your Spirit to be with us in this hour.

Does any theistic Christian think that God's Spirit might not be present at any time or place? Obviously we are inviting the *people* to open up to that spirit.

Dear God, please be with the leaders of our nation, and of all the world's nations, that they may be led to work for a more just and peaceful world.

Does any theistic Christian think that God is not already calling these people toward such visions?

Dear Parent in heaven, as elders in your church, commissioned in the name of Jesus Christ, we call upon you for the blessing of healing for this person who is suffering so greatly.

Do any of us seriously imagine that a perfectly loving divine Parent would wait to be asked before doing everything possible to ease the suffering of God's children, or would care who offers such a prayer? Would God only listen if the right people with the right priesthood and the right morality were to ask in the right way?

Clearly, few Christians, if any, mean what is implied by many of the words we say in prayer. Surely Christians do not think that God sits back passively, doing nothing, until some human being begs for a favor in a sufficiently groveling way. Nor do we take seriously the biblical images of a God who must be handled like a raging bull—as is suggested in the images of Abraham or Moses pleading with Yahweh not to unleash his fury. So why do we pray as if we did? To alert God to a problem that God might otherwise miss? Do we hope to change God's mind? To change God's values? To persuade God to be more helpful than God would otherwise be?

Such a reflection very quickly leads us to recognize that we pray to change ourselves, not God. Prayer, even in traditional theologies, is an act of worship. And the primary purpose of worship is to center our lives around that which we consider to be worthy of such commitment. Prayer should be an act whereby we center ourselves around and align ourselves with the sacred.

You don't have to be a process theologian to recognize that prayer should change us, not God. This obvious fact has been obscured, however, by the inconsistency between our images of God as all-loving and as unilaterally all-powerful. If God is loving God must surely seek to ease suffering. But if God is all-powerful then God has obviously chosen not to relieve the actual suffering that exists. So our prayer of healing, which presupposes that God can simply heal whenever God wishes, must also suppose that God has so far chosen *not* to do so. Our prayer, then, becomes an effort to change God's mind, or perhaps to satisfy some strange law God has that God will only act lovingly—will only relieve suffering or be present with us or speak to national leaders—if the right people with the right theology and right authority ask in just the right way, perhaps "in Jesus' name, Amen."

What if we really imagine God as loving, so that God is already doing everything within God's power to work for the good long before it has occurred to us to ask? How then would we pray? How would we pray to a God who is already always present, loving, calling, working? How would we pray to the God envisioned in process theology?

God, Prayer, and the Life of the World

Before talking about how we should pray, it may be good to review the process understanding of the world and God. This world is a world of experience, organized into increasingly complex creatures with richer experience. God shares the experience of each creature, and each creature experiences God. This is God's omnipresence. Each creature's experience of God is an experience of possibilties and of a call appropriate to that creature.

In process thought there is no absolute line between life and nonlife, although there are crucial boundaries at which major differences arise. For example, there is no metaphysical difference between a dog and a person. Both seem to experience and react in a unified way, with some degree of consciousness and some common emotions. But human beings are so much more complex that our minds appear to cross a crucial boundary into the ability to handle abstractions, making possible science, literature, and morality. We have more of what dogs have. But it is a crucial degree of more.

In the same way, the difference between living organisms and those organic molecules that hover on the edge of life is a matter of degree. But it is a degree that is crucial. From the process perspective, the crucial difference between them (which is made possible by the kind of structural differences a biologist could describe) is that living creatures have a vastly greater capacity for novel responses to their environment. Life is a function of novelty—of freedom. And since, process theologians hold, God is the ground of freedom, God is also the ground of life. It is God who, in each moment, is the foundation of life in every living creature.

Process theism is not pantheism—the view that the world is God. Rather it is pan*en*theism—the view that the world is *in* God, and also that God is *in* all things in the world. We are surrounded by a world in which God is at work giving and sustaining life. God cannot *control* that life, but God can and does act to nurture and support it. In each blade of grass, in each cell of our bodies, God is already present and active.

Understanding the world, God, and life in this way must change the way we think about everything. We can no longer see God as concerned only with human beings, much less only with us or our narrow group. Process theologians are extremely sympathetic with those who cry out for the welfare of whales and dolphins and other creatures. Process theologians see God as present, as living, in the entire world of plants and animals.

So when we pray to God, we pray to that which is already in us and around us, already at work to make our prayer possible, already calling us toward health and love and life. What shall we say to such a God?

Remember that prayer is an act of worship in which we seek to center ourselves, to align ourselves, to be sensitive and responsive. Prayer is primarily for us. So when we ask what we should say, we are asking how we shall speak to ourselves and to each other in our efforts to center, align, listen, and respond to the sacred.

Prayer and Liberation

Part of the answer lies in silence. We must listen. Part of our answer lies in action. We must change the world that obscures God's voice. But changing the world involves changing ourselves. In changing ourselves we change what God can do. For God can work with us when we are loving in ways God cannot work with us when we are hateful. Thus changing ourselves does literally change what God can do in this world. Similarly, changing any part of the world changes what God can do. God cannot work with people who are starving or beaten or drugged in the same ways God can work with them when their lives are freer. By changing the world we change the range of possibilities for both God and the world.

Much prayer is directed toward persuading people to accept the will of God. That, of course, remains important. Shortsighted creatures that we are, we do not share God's infinite experience. So process theists also remind us that we need to listen for God's call and try to capture a larger vision—which may mean changing our hopes and expectations.

All too often, however, prayers have called people to accept an oppressive status quo. Prayers have admonished people to accept their poverty or their oppression as God's will. Process theology certainly rejects that. Process theology calls, instead, for prayers of liberation through silence, words, and actions. Liberating human minds, hearts, and bodies also liberates God to act more effectively in the world.

Here again, we must remember that we can do things God cannot do. We can carry picket signs. We can vote. We can stand up and speak against injustice. We can recycle paper and plastic and cans. We can design and build more efficient energy systems. We can decide to do with less so that others may have more. By our actions we can create a better world in which God can offer better possibilities.

Prayer can change what God can do. Process theists believe this. Prayer may be seen then as a whole range of activities in which we work cooperatively with God to create a better world within which God can offer better possibilities and do better things, within which God can be better perceived and better responded to.

Finally, however, remember that true prayer changes us. We all want to believe that we are the ones really responding to God's call, that we are the ones on God's side, that we are the ones enlightening the world by speaking for God. But that is rarely so. We never have a direct access to God that is not interwoven with our own human desires, selfishness, shortsightedness, and personal circumstance. Our perception of

God's will is always historically conditioned—shaped by our society, culture, biology, finances, politics, sexuality, family, etc. So continued prayer and self-critical repentance, continual openness to the insights of others and to new insights of our own are all essential components of a life of prayer. We must continually seek our own liberation if we are to liberate the world.

Prayer and Healing

Most process theologians would also want to say something about the ways in which our relatedness with all of this world of experience may have implications for the power of our prayers. There is some—certainly inconclusive—evidence that living cells are sensitive to other living cells around them, that all life shares in a common "field" that ties it together. Normally our connections are very tenuous, very trivial. We rarely, if ever, can read other minds directly.

But it is conspicuous that we are tied in many ways to the living cells in our own bodies. Some of these ties are strong, specific, and direct. We can move our arms and wink our eyes. Other connections are less direct and precise. The beating of our heart is part of the involuntary nervous system. It is easier to raise our heart beat through the voluntary exercise of the muscles than by meditating. But it is possible to learn to influence the heart in other ways. In the same way, our minds are connected to many of the cells in our bodies in ways that are so indirect, so imprecise, that it is nearly impossible for us to affect them by mere efforts of will. Despite a few dramatic stories, we have very little success at wishing cancer cells away.

The point, however, is that cancer cells and viruses are living things within our bodies, and that there is compelling evidence that some states of mind make our bodies more vulnerable to their destructive effects than others. It is not all or nothing. It is not natural versus supernatural. It is not simply a case where either our minds have no effect or they have total control. It is not a question of "faith." Rather, we have a wide range of degrees to which our minds can influence living cells within the body. Once we turn to cells outside our own bodies, then our connections with them obviously drop dramatically, though perhaps not entirely.

These views have several implications. Process thinkers would be among those who assume that as we learn more—and learn new ways to learn—we may hope that we can become better at healing our bodies with our minds—and our minds with our bodies. And prayer here would mean working with God to do what God is already doing—calling us to health. It may well be that we can become better at praying in this way—especially if we stop thinking that prayer is an effort to get God to do what God otherwise would not do.

Another implication is that there is no direct contest between healing by prayer or through other methods. If aspirin cures headaches then there is no reason why we shouldn't take aspirin. If we can eventually learn to cure headaches more quickly without aspirin, then all the better. But there is no reason to abandon what works until we find something that works better. Taking an aspirin doesn't show some lack of faith in God's healing power. It is just another way of helping God bring about healing—a way that God cannot utilize alone. God can't take the aspirin for us.

It is obvious, then, that process theologians are going to be sympathetic with imaging, laughter, meditation, and other strategies for learning about the powers of mind to work with our bodies. But they would say that we cannot know in advance just what is possible. It may be that there are very severe limits, inherent in the nature of our bodies and minds, to what mental healing can do. Or, it may be that there are enormous powers of mind over matter that we have not yet even imagined. These are contingent questions, awaiting trial and error investigation.

Conclusion

Prayer makes a lot of sense in process theology. It is not magic or supernatural. It is not an effort to change God's mind. It is an effort to change ourselves and the world in cooperation with God, to do what God cannot do so that God can do God's work more effectively. God is never lagging behind needing to be prodded by our prayers. Rather, God is always ahead of us, always calling us, always waiting for us to respond.

CHAPTER 16

Miracles

"The miracle of birth" is a wise phrase, pointing us toward a healthy theology of miracles. Birth is not supernatural. It involves no divine intervention violating natural processes. We know a tremendous amount about reproduction and may one day be able to create life in laboratories. Yet for all that, we still feel, and speak of, the miracle of birth.

Proclaiming the miracle of birth expresses our wonder and awe. But even more, it declares our sense that there is something sacred here. In a child's birth we are confronted with something that really matters, that grabs us and shakes us, centering our lives on fundamental values and revealing to us what is worthy of our ultimate commitment. A birth changes everything. In all of these ways, birth is miraculous.

Miracles becomes problems when we think of them as demonstrating divine power to intervene in the world however God wishes. The problems are not merely scientific, but also theological and moral. Nothing challenges the goodness of God or the justice of the universe more than the stark randomness of such alleged "miracles." In what follows I want to explain several problems with the idea of supernatural miracles and to explain why process theology offers a better option.

Justice and Kindness

Joy and a sense of gratitude are appropriate responses to an unexpected healing or dramatic rescue from danger. We all rejoice with those who are so fortunate. But nothing makes God seem more cruel and unjust than the idea that God miraculously saved one plane passenger in a crash that killed a hundred. Inevitably we must ask, "Why save this one while millions suffer and die every day?" The injustice is multiplied if we attribute the alleged "miracle" to special worthiness or divine love, since we then imply that everyone else is less worthy or less loved by God. The entire book of Job is an anguished witness to the obvious fact that the world does not consistently reward righteousness or punish sin. Job, like billions of others, was innocent, and yet he suffered—and asked why.

Obviously, when good people shout with joy that they have been amazingly healed, they do not intend to condemn others. Yet, just a little thought must show us what it feels like for the many who do not experience such good fortune. "If God healed your child, why not mine? Is your child more worthy than mine? Does God love your child more than mine? Is God punishing my child for my sins?" Few sensitive people mean to suggest such a picture of God. But when we fail to think about the implications of our theology, we can really hurt those around us. A careless theology of miracles can be cruelly unkind.

Science, Chance, and the God of the Gaps

The moral reasons for rejecting the idea of miracles as supernatural interventions by God are strongly reinforced by just a little reflection on what we know of history, science, and the world about us.

Lightning was believed to be the weapon of many ancient gods. And no wonder. Lightning is powerful, awesome, potentially devastating, and totally beyond the understanding of prescientific peoples. Most of us still don't really understand it exactly, but we learn as children that it is a natural electrical discharge having nothing to do with Zeus or Thor. More important, perhaps, we control the power of electricity dozen of times each day as we flip lights on and off with a touch of the finger. The gods who threw lightning bolts are gone now. If we tie our God to lightning or anything like it, our God will gradually go away, too.

There will, of course, always be events we do not yet understand. The universe is too large, too complex for us to know it all. Consequently, there will always be people saying that God is found in those gaps in our knowledge. But this "god of the gaps" idea is demeaning to God and deadly to theology. It presents a god hiding in the shadows of our ignorance, shrinking before the light of human knowledge and intelligence. Such a god grows smaller as our knowledge grows larger.

Consider how little we know of the mind's power to heal the body. Everyone knows that bodies and minds interact. Apparently anxiety, stress, and depression can contribute to physical symptoms ranging from cold sores to cancer. It is hardly surprising then that doctors increasingly see a healthy attitude as part of the treatment for bodily diseases. But we know little of how this all works. So when prayer helps a person relax and feel loved and hopeful, we find it easy to see supernatural causes for the physical improvement this can bring. But what will happen when, as seems likely, we learn how to train people to heal themselves, at least partly, with their minds? What happens when mental healing is no more mysterious than lightning is now? What were once called "faith" healings may become as ordinary and secular as electric lights.

Chance also challenges the idea of supernatural miracles. By definition, most people have "normal" intelligence, size, or height. A few are brillant or retarded, small or large, short or tall. Exceptions to the norm are regularly noted in all domains of human experience. There is nothing any more supernatural about Einstein's genius or a seven foot basketball player than about the tragedy of a child whose mental or physical growth is stunted. In exactly the same way, some people who get cancer will die faster than anyone expects, leaving us in shocked dismay. Most, by definition, will follow a more "normal" course. A very few will recover quickly to the amazement of all. Because we are grateful for the surprising recovery, we may honor it with the name *miracle*. But was the recovery any more supernatural than the death or the "normal" case?

Healthy faith cannot depend on ignorance. A balanced view of the world cannot be built by crediting God with a few of the more favorable chance events. Knowledge of God and knowledge of the world must never be enemies.

Process Theology

The moral problems with miracles arise when we assume that God can do whatever God wants. The scientific problems come when we separate a few unusual events as "acts of God" in violation of natural processes. Can we formulate a vision of divine power in which God's activity and love are expressed throughout nature? With the question of miracles before us, let us consider once again how process theologians believe God acts in the world.

Perhaps, as modern physics suggests to some of us, agency of a sort is present even in the smallest, subatomic events composing the natural process. Perhaps, then, God's power is necessarily persuasive rather than coercive. Process theologians envision God as presenting the possibilities that make freedom meaningful, and as calling us toward the better choices. God's activity can be seen, then, as the foundation that makes it possible for the world to combine order with freedom, life, and adventure.

Morally, we can picture a divine love so great that in all events in every moment God is doing everything within God's power to bring about good, eagerly calling for the cooperation of all who will respond. But God works with a world in which agency is both fundamental and irrevocable, so that God cannot force the world's decisions. Scientifically, we can see here a God acting in *everything*, so that there are no *isolated* events that are "acts of God" standing outside the course of nature. The crucial vision here is of divine power as always present and active, but as always, inescapably interwoven with the causal forces of the world.

In this vision, God wishes and works to heal every diseased cell, to draw us away from every hateful thought. But neither the world nor we can be coerced by God. So we, with God, can rightfully celebrate when prayer and intelligence and good fortune combine to make the world more responsive to God's call. But even when the worst happens we can affirm that God is present with us, grieving with us, and working with us to create whatever good is possible out of the genuine evil we confront.

In the process vision of things, God has been working patiently with the world all along. It was not possible for divine power to simply create a world that was free of disease. And most of the creatures of the world are incapable of responding to any vision of such a world. Health, kindness, and self-sacrifice have no relevance to elementary particles. Human beings, however, are vastly more capable of catching such a divine vision, and so it is with human beings that God has the best means of working in the world to bring about healing.

However ambivalent we may feel about modern science, we can hardly fail to see how absolutely amazing it is that in the last few decades we have actually acquired the power to free humankind from many of the dread plagues that have ravished people for millennia. In the developed nations diseases like typhoid, typhus, malaria, polio, measles, whooping cough, and dysentery have disappeared or been largely controlled. Small pox, a terrible killer, has been entirely defeated. People who would once have died from heart attacks now live long and healthy lives. And the "miracles" of modern medicine extend beyond preventing and curing diseases. My daughter's elbow injury as a small child would have left her with a withered arm had not doctors learned how to repair splintered bone.

We have much yet to learn and many challenges to meet. Even our very success at saving lives creates problems in population increase and dignified lives for older citizens. But we can hardly fail to rejoice at the ways in which our growth of knowledge enables people (who have access to it) to live longer and healthier lives. From the perspective of process theology, we can see this as a direct reflection of God's patient calling throughout the history of the race. God may not be able to persuade many cancer cells in many bodies to restructure themselves, but God may be able to call people in this time to learn how to cure cancer. We are God's hands in much of the work God wishes to do.

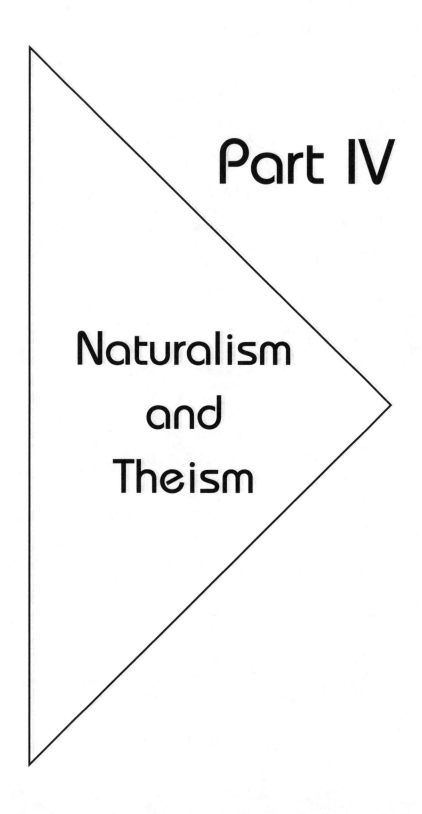

Part IV

Naturalism and Theism

Introduction
to Part IV

Millions of Christians in the twentieth century have come to think of divinity or sacredness apart from belief in a divine being. Paul Tillich changed Christian theology for many by insisting that "God" does not "exist" (is not one being among other beings), but is rather a symbolic name for the ground of all existence, "the ground of being." Bishop Robinson's small classic, *Honest to God*, challenged millions of readers to grow beyond belief in a God who was "out there." Bonhoeffer wanted a "religionless Christianity" in which we stood "before God without God." Some "Death of God" theologians sought for a purely secular, notheistic interpretation of the Christian gospel.

Some people enthusiastic about the possibilities of process thought have asked me whether a similar shift in religious

125

perspective might not work in process theology just as well. Could we, they ask, preserve the values of the process-relational vision—its reconception of power and value, its focus on process and relatedness, its openness to the value of non-human life, its appreciation of feminism, and its positive response to the ambiguity of life—while finding sacredness entirely within the world of natural processes? The answer, I believe, is yes. There are many naturalists, including myself, who do find a meaningful religious worldview based on process-relational thought without the idea of a divine being.

This concluding section contains two chapters. In the first, I will briefly explain and explore the concept of "process naturalism" as a religious perspective grounded in the process-relational vision, but without the divine Subject of process theism. As part of this I will introduce ideas from Henry Nelson Wieman, who was a leading spokesperson for reconceiving religion within this framework.

In the final chapter, however, John B. Cobb, Jr., whom I view as the pre-eminent process theologian, has graciously agreed to reflect on three questions. Why do we need God to make sense of the world in the process-relational vision? What difference does the process God make in the world of our experience? What are other contributions that process thought can make beyond those discussed in this book?

CHAPTER 17

Process
Naturalism

First, let me define *naturalism* as the view that nature is what there is—all that there is. There is no being or subject apart from or transcendent to the natural processes themselves. There is no ground for the world's creative advance other than the world itself. A religious naturalist would hold that whatever we define as sacred, whatever we understand as good or evil, is part of nature.

It is important to repeat, however, that process theism is not a form of supernaturalism either. So the difference between the two positions is not naturalism vs. supernaturalism, but the question of whether the world of finite, natural creatures is unified in such a way as to give rise to a single divine Subject. When I speak of process naturalism, I mean the view that there is no such divine Subject of all experience. There is just the world of finite creatures.

127

Second, the difference is not about whether we speak of God. Many process naturalists, like Henry Nelson Wieman, do use religious language, including God-language, to describe their vision of reality and values. Many naturalists, however, do not. So while I would want to describe process naturalists as those who envision reality without the unifying divine consciousness affirmed by process theists, it would be misleading to say that all naturalists reject God-language.

Finally, the common ground between process-relational theism and naturalism is substantial. Many of the problems in traditional religious thought that process naturalists have challenged are also challenged by process theists. Also, most of the virtues of process-relational naturalism that I shall discuss are shared quite enthusiastically by process theists.

Naturalism and Sacredness

Naturalism can include a sense of sacredness. In naturalism, sacredness is not something derived from a supernatural or divine source that impinges on our world from outside. Sacredness is not a magical or mystical quality something might or might not acquire. It isn't a thing or stuff. It is primarily a way of experiencing the world.

Sometimes people have very powerful experiences in which they suddenly understand and feel what really matters—at least to them. Theists of various kinds have often said that God is omnipresent. Some thoughtful theologians have suggested that what this means is that any thing or any event in the world could be the medium by which we are opened up to an encounter with God. If we simply replace "God" with "a powerful sense of what really matters to us," then a naturalist can agree. And with the theist, we can affirm these experiences as moments in which we discover what is sacred.

In my own religious language, I would say that I experience my wife and children as sacred. This means to me, first, that they themselves are of ultimate importance to me. But at the same time, they also act as powerful symbols for, or windows through which I see, the importance of all children, all people, and to some degree, all life. Their sacredness does not depend upon any divinity outside themselves, yet they participate in a realm of value extending throughout my natural world.

Secondarily, I might speak of other things as sacred, too: an act of self-sacrifice, the beauty of a symphony, or the quest for truth. Someone might experience this same sacredness in communion with objects of nature like a mountain, tree, or lake. In any case, the same kind of experiences of sacredness that theists think of as revelations of a divine being can be familiar to naturalists despite different explanations of their origins or ultimate referents.

Sacredness is not purely a subjective matter, however. Naturalists can also link sacredness with language about transcendence. Jerome Stone suggests that it may be helpful to think of some dimensions of the world as "relatively transcendent." Although not transcendent to the natural world, they do exercise a sort of relative transcendence within the world. "By a relatively transcendent norm I mean any value that continually transcends in worth and claim any attempt to attain it, indeed to formulate it with precision."[1]

> Truth is a paradigm of a continually challenging norm. No matter what level of understanding is achieved, truth continues to function as a goal in relation to which our theories are but approximations. The truth is an ideal, never fully attained, which functions as a continual demand that we push toward that goal.... Thus truth functions as a continually transcendent demand. Likewise the pursuit of other humane goals such as beauty, moral goodness and justice are pursuits of continually transcendent demands.[2]

These comments suggest some ways in which naturalistic thinkers may still wish to use some of the language traditionally claimed by theistic traditions. We, too, *experience* and *conceive* of the world in ways that give words like *sacred* and *transcendent* meaning and force. But we see them as applying to the realms of nature and history.

---

[1]Jerome A. Stone, "The Viability of Religious Naturalism," pp. 3–4, unpublished paper.

[2]*Ibid.*, p. 4, but cited by him from Jerome A. Stone, "A Minimal Model of Transcendence," *American Journal of Theology and Philosophy*, Vol. 8, No. 3 (Sept. 1977), p. 129f.

A Process-relational Naturalism

Our present focus, however, is on a specifically process naturalism. Given process thought's dynamic view of nature, what happens if we accept the process vision of reality without the God of process theism? How would we see the world if we were process naturalists? In large part, the virtues of process theism that we already have explored will remain in a religious process naturalism.

For process naturalists, process and relatedness are still the combined starting points for all things. We still see the world in creative process as the becoming and perishing of interrelated moments of experience. In this sense the universe remains deeply spiritual. Those values to which feminists and environmentalists have helped draw our attention are still basic. Connectedness and wholeness are fundamental rather than independence and atomism. Relational power rather than unilateral power remains the most appropriate approach to social existence.

Process naturalism shares with process theism a recognition of the ambiguity of all existence. The same actions, events, and structures may give rise to both pain and pleasure, both destruction and creation. No particular state of affairs is "the way things were intended to be," because there is no divine Creator to intend anything. Slavery, sexism, and homophobia, for example, are seen as arising from human self-centeredness and prejudice, and do not reflect any divine moral command. So process naturalism also escapes those particular oppressive tendencies that so easily emerge from some religious visions.

Process naturalists also see us as sharing in depths of experience. Sense experience, while our primary focus, is only a sharper, clearer, more abstract product of vaguer, more primal experiences in our bodily cells. The world is a rich and amazing place, and we have much to learn about it and our place within it. Since process naturalists also believe that bodies and minds are unified, they would also predict that we have much to learn about the powers of the mind to heal our bodies (and vice versa), and each others' minds and bodies. But being empiricists, they remind us that we must not make rash leaps into unjustified claims. Trial and error will be as necessary here as in any scientific inquiry.

Process naturalists would bring to bear the same basic philosophy of committed relativism that is able to embrace diversity without abandoning ethical judgments. With or without God, ethical judgments must be grounded in actual processes—physical, biological, psychological, and social. As far as these are shared we may look for common foundations for our values. As these vary, values may, too.

Similarly, the positive appreciation of religious, cultural, ethnic, and personal pluralism would be affirmed. The world is really richer for these diversities, provided that we approach them openly and creatively. We should be glad that not everyone is a Christian, or a Jew, or a Buddhist, because these different religions have enabled us to explore and preserve a wider range of values and traditions than any one religion could.

Ecological diversity, too, would be a positive value embraced by process-relational naturalists. The world is filled with value-enjoying life beyond the human. To diminish that diversity is not only to threaten our survival, but the richness of our own lives as participants in that ecological society.

Process naturalists would observe that once people get past the shock of viewing the world without reference to a divine being, the daily conduct of life and ethics is essentially unaffected. Largely, we still feel the same pains and pleasures, joys and sorrows, fears and hopes for this life. We are not changed in our need for food, shelter, or love. Indeed, the reasons for our ethical judgments may be even clearer.

Consider, for example, the need to work for peace. Should we work for peace because God tells us to, or the scriptures say so, or because Jesus is called the Prince of Peace? Is this why we should work for peace? Isn't the real reason we should work for peace simply that peace is a better way to live, because it is healthier for children and other living things?

Process naturalism shares virtually every value and every ethical standard with process theism, and many of these are shared with Christianity and other religions. The only difference is that process naturalists see these values as rooted entirely within the natural processes themselves, as temporal, contingent, and ambiguous as they may be. In the world in which we actually live, we should love one another, seek justice, and work for peace because we are all inseparably related in the creative advance.

God

What would it mean for a nontheistic naturalist to speak of "God"? One important vision comes from Henry Nelson Wieman. Wieman argued that we have usually misconceived the nature of the religious quest. We have thought that it was a question about whether or not to believe in some predefined notion of a divine being. The question of faith is then the problem of whether such belief is to be based on revelation, authority, intuition, or on evidence and reason.

Before we can speak appropriately of "God," Wieman argued, we must be clearer about the nature of religion. Religion is a quest for salvation from the evils of life. Most fundamentally, religion is a quest for human transformation. Human beings are capable of being transformed toward great good or great evil. People can be kind and loving, finding joy in lives of service to others, but people can also run concentration camps. What makes the difference? What saves us? Within this context Wieman radically recast the question of "God."

> The word "God" is irrelevant to the religious problem unless the word is used to refer to whatever in truth operates to save people from evil and to the greater good no matter *how much this operating reality may differ from all traditional ideas about it.*[3]

Wieman's definition does not tell us what the source of human good is. It does not rule out the possibility that it may indeed be a divine being like that described in the preceding chapters. But Wieman was convinced that the source of human good (and, indeed, the good of nonhuman creatures as well) must lie within the natural world.

Wieman pointed to the obvious fact that whatever affects us must exist within the world of our experience. We are nurtured by healthy foods, loving parents and friends, proper education, justice, and peace. We are harmed by abuse, poverty, starvation, disease, oppression, and violence. There is nothing supernatural about any of these. Good and bad alike, they are all products of our natural and social world processes

---

[3]Henry Nelson Wieman, *Man's Ultimate Commitment* (Southern Illinois University Press, 1974), p. 12 (first published 1958). Out of respect for Wieman's commitment to creative change, I have edited his remarks to remove sexist language, which was still unchallenged when he was writing (emphasis his).

that must be combated within nature and society. Wieman, we might say, agreed with the biblical conviction that "God"—that which transforms us away from evil and toward the good—acts in history.

Unlike process theism, many forms of religion deny the importance of this world. They seek for salvation in a timeless realm and see the ultimate sources of good as utterly beyond temporal events. Wieman asserted that those who call us to look toward some utterly timeless and transcendental realm to seek what saves us from evil and leads us toward good are, however unintentionally, harming us by diverting our attention from what really matters. Worse, in a time when we have the power to destroy our world, religion that seeks salvation as escape from this world is dangerous.

It is as though a man performing a surgical operation were to deny that the vital organs are in the body at all. Only their temporal manifestations are there, he says, but, since they themselves are not there, no cutting of the knife can seriously hurt them. Such a man should never be allowed to perform a capital operation.[4]

We live in the world of nature. Process naturalists believe that nature is what there is. This means that the sources of human good must lie within nature, too. That is where we must look and work.

Many religious visions include a very healthy and vital sense that we serve God best by serving our neighbors. Process naturalists want to say something very simple about this. What really helps children become the best they can be happens right here and now: good food, loving parents and friends, strong role models, good medical care, sound education, justice, and peace. With or without a transcendent divinity, these are the things that matter. Yet, there is so much about nature and humanity and the sources of good and evil that we do not yet understand. Wieman and other process naturalists call us to focus our religious commitment on these questions.

---

[4]Wieman, *The Source of Human Good* (Southern Illinois University Press, 1967), p. 35 (first published 1948).

CHAPTER 18

Process Theism

by
John B. Cobb, Jr.

Bob Mesle is an extraordinary thinker. He has a deep, sympathetic, and accurate understanding of process theism, yet he himself believes that process thought of a nontheistic variety can capture all the values of process theism while avoiding entanglement in its dubious speculation. Nevertheless, he is quite willing to give a process theist the last word!

As he notes, the line between "process naturalism" and "process theism" is not easy to draw. I, for example, often call myself <u>a naturalistic theist</u> or <u>a theistic naturalist</u>. Furthermore, some people who call themselves theists hold just the same beliefs as others who reject theism. They simply disagree as to what it means to be a theist.

Mesle recognizes that it is particularly hard to say whether Henry Nelson Wieman is a "theist" or a "naturalist." He fits

Mesle's definition of naturalism and yet he emphatically affirms the reality of God. Wieman became a naturalist for the sake of faith in God! For him what is of supreme importance is that people give themselves in trust and devotion to God. But as long as God's reality is in dispute, this unqualified trust and devotion is hardly possible. He concluded that the reality of God must be established indubitably, so that instead of debating God's existence, we would see that the real decision is whether to serve God or not.

As Mesle makes clear, Wieman understood God as an actual process, operative in nature and especially in human community. With great insight and precision, he described that process through which human good grows. It is the process through which we are creatively transformed. He showed that this process cannot be controlled or directed by the human will because it is the process that transforms the will. It cannot be subordinated to human purposes because it transforms human purposes. If our will and purposes are to be creatively transformed, then we must trust this process and allow it to reshape us without knowing what the results will be.

In traditional Christian language, Wieman teaches that we are saved by grace and not by works. That is, our creative transformation is not our own work. We can place ourselves in situations in which it is more likely to occur and open ourselves to it. We cannot do it to ourselves or make it happen. We are saved by grace alone through faith.

Mesle has asked me to say what difference belief in God makes within the context of process thought. Wieman's belief in God makes a difference with respect to our fundamental stance in life. If human beings are the supreme realities, then the usual response, even of process thinkers, is to think in terms of intelligent planning, organizing, and controlling of events for human benefit. Of course, all this has a place. But I believe, with Wieman, that the deeper truth is that we need to find that which is trustworthy and to trust it even when we do not know where this will lead.

A process naturalist such as Mesle, who does not focus on that one process that creates and redeems, may serve it nevertheless. Indeed, I believe that he does. But the tendency of process naturalism is not to focus on trust and devotion to God. Hence I suggest that in general a difference between those for whom *God* is important and those for whom this word is dispensable is the strong belief of the former that we do not make ourselves or generate our own good, that trusting and self-giving are more fundamental even than taking responsibility for our own beliefs and actions, and that for this reason determining what to trust is a very important matter.

Wieman distinguished that which is worthy of ultimate trust and devotion from all else. This distinction is very important to him. To trust absolutely what is not worthy of such trust or to devote ourselves unreservedly to what is not worthy of such devotion is "idolatry."

Wieman identifies the process that always and everywhere makes for human good as the "creative good." He contrasts this with "created goods." The former is the process through which good things come into being. The latter are the good things that come into being through that process. These include rich human relationships, ongoing communities and institutions, and profound wisdom. These are very precious; if they were not, there would be no reason to give such devotion to the process that brings them into being. But to treat even the best of them as if they were sacred or worthy of ultimate devotion is dangerous and destructive.

People can disagree as to whether focusing attention on the distinction between God and creatures is desirable or undesirable. But that Wieman's belief in God has practical effects seems evident to me. Wieman discussed these effects in some detail in relation to education, to government, and to the world of business, as well as to the religious life.

Wieman's thought has been important to me since my days as a graduate student. God's reality had become very uncertain for me, and I found my doubts very troubling indeed. What Wieman identified as God was not all that *God* had meant to me; so I was not satisfied. But Wieman showed to my satisfaction, then and now, that careful examination of human experience reveals the reality of a creative process that is worthy of our trust and devotion. In our time that is a very great accomplishment.

Wieman is one of the main sources of process theism. He developed this theism in the context of radical empiricism. Meanwhile, a colleague at Chicago was developing a profoundly different sort of process theism. His name was Charles Hartshorne. It is Hartshorne's form of process theism that

Mesle has in mind when he makes his distinction of process naturalism and process theism. Unlike Wieman, Hartshorne understands that *God* identifies the all-inclusive mind, experience, or soul.

Hartshorne suggests that we think of the relation of God and the world as like that of the psyche or soul to the body, or most particularly to the brain. Hartshorne thinks of each cell in the brain in each moment as an individual subject that receives from others and in turn acts on others. Each cellular event or experience is also taken up into the unified experience of the human person. This experience is not just made up of all the cellular experiences added one to another. Instead it integrates them into a single coherent experience with its own memories and anticipations. Similarly, all of these human (and other creaturely) experiences are taken up into the unified cosmic experience that is God.

Hartshorne calls this doctrine "panentheism." All things are in God. This is different from "pantheism," which means that all things together *are* God. In terms of the analogy of soul to brain, pantheism would be like "psycho-physical identism." This is the philosophical doctrine that the psyche or soul is the same thing as the brain, just viewed in a different way.

Hartshorne believes that the soul has a subjective unity of its own such that a human experience is quite different from that of the cells individually or collectively. Similarly God has a subjective unity such that the divine experience is quite different from that of the creatures who contribute to it even when all of those are added together.

Mesle asks whether this way of thinking of God as including the world but as more than the world makes an important difference to human life. Cannot all the values that this doctrine provides be had without it?

At first this question seems strange to those of us who find panentheism deeply meaningful. But a little reflection helps us understand it. We are not led by this belief in God to expect anything to happen in the world that is different from what others expect. Some people think that unless belief in God justifies expectation of divine intervention, such belief can make no difference.

I am sure that Mesle does not limit differences to these cruder versions. He means also making a difference in the lives of believers. Here it seems evident to panentheistic believers that our belief does make a difference. Yet in the way we explain our belief, we open the door to denying that it makes a difference in this sense either. We need to look at this more carefully.

The problem arises because process theists tend not to take expressions of disbelief at face value. We think that the ways people act and feel imply some beliefs that they may consciously deny. Since in some sense even unbelievers are believers, one can ask: What difference does conscious belief make?

This is not quite so paradoxical as it sounds. I'll illustrate it with respect to two other beliefs before we apply it to belief in God. We can ask in each case whether, even though the belief may operate even when it is ignored or denied, conscious affirmation still makes a difference.

One example is that the future will, in general terms, be much like the past—that is, that the same structures of nature will continue to operate. All science is based on this belief, and for just this reason the belief is rarely, if ever, stated as a scientific one. Scientists get along fine without even thinking about this belief. The same is true of all of our planning for the future.

Still we can ask whether this expectation of continuity is justified. If it is not, then our attitudes and activities are placed in profound question. Process thought argues that the expectation *is* justified. This is because each event occurs as it does primarily because of its inclusion of past events. This ensures that it will be continuous in basic ways with the past.

Many people do not accept this theory. Yet they continue to believe that the future will be like the past. They are so sure of this that they feel no need to have any supporting theory at all. For most purposes they get along just as well without concerning themselves about the justification of their assumptions.

Even in this case we cannot say that the theory makes no difference at all. Reflective questions arise here and there to which this theory provides an answer. This answer leads to different results from others. For example, it enables us to see how there can be change as well as continuity. Nevertheless, I offer this example as a case where confidence in the fact is so deep-seated and so rarely doubted that the theory that justifies it makes very little practical difference in life, although it does give some satisfaction to those who hold it.

A second example is the view that to some extent people are responsible for how they act. That implies that human beings make decisions they are not forced to make—that is, that there is human freedom. But human freedom is very hard to explain, and many people, especially philosophers, deny it intellectually. Process thinkers believe that even those who deny it explicitly still believe it at some level of their being and continue to act in terms of this belief rather than in terms of the complete determinism they avow.

In this case, too, we can ask whether the conscious belief in human freedom makes any difference. At one level, the answer is no. People act freely and treat others as if they were free whether they affirm it or not. Still, in this area what one consciously believes *does* make a difference. Those who deny that human beings are free are likely to accept less responsibility for their own decisions as time goes by. Also, distinguishing what we are responsible for and what we are not responsible for is discouraged if we suppose that all our actions are determined. Existentialists pointed out how deterministic thinking can lead to a spectator relation to life rather than one of engagement.

With these analogies in mind, let us return to panentheism. Among other things, panentheism is a theory that explains why there is an ineradicable sense that what happens in the world matters. We can think of this as a theory analogous to the one about how the past enters into the future and so ensures that the future will be continuous with the past. Just as everyone believes that the future will be like the past, whether or not they adopt this theory, so everyone believes that what happens in the world has importance, whether or not they subscribe to any theory that justifies this belief.

I need to explain the connection panentheists see between God and our sense of the importance of what happens in the world. Every event has a certain importance in and for itself just as it occurs. But this is very ephemeral indeed. Pain and pleasure, enjoyment and misery, pass as soon as they come into being. Fame and power are equally fleeting. To justify the worthwhileness of patient action, we often put the emphasis upon its consequences for oneself and others. But these consequences are just as transitory. These reflections lead some to the explicit belief in the futility and meaninglessness of actions—indeed, of life itself.

Nevertheless, even those who come to these conclusions characteristically feel it is worthwhile to share them with others. In any case, they continue to act as if it mattered what they do. At some fundamental level of their being, their actions testify to a conviction that what happens does matter, however transitory the events and however minimal their effects in the course of history. That implies that it matters to One whose being is not transitory, One who is everlasting.

The modern history of the West attests to some such connection between God and human meaning. The revolt against God was often a revolt against attention to another world at the expense of this one. It was motivated by a strong sense of the meaning and importance of life here and now. Yet when belief in God faded, there arose the question of the basis of meaning and importance. Nihilism became a fundamental spiritual threat.

Nevertheless, without conscious belief in such a One, many people still unquestioningly think that what happens in their own lives and in the lives of others matters a great deal. They do not experience nihilism as a threat. For them, the situation is like that with respect to belief that the future will be like the past. The belief in meaning and importance is so secure that theories that justify it are of little interest.

On the other hand, the comments I have made about recent history indicate that this is not the whole story. People who do not believe in God can also come to the conscious belief that life has no meaning. This is more like the second example of belief that human beings are not free. Those who hold these beliefs still act in many ways as if they believed in meaning and freedom. But the conscious rejection of these beliefs still has profound effects. It is hard to question that nihilistic tendencies have played a growing role in Western society to the detriment of us all.

I do not mean to assert that process naturalists are nihilists! I detect no note of this sort in Mesle's writings. Indeed, I do not sense that he experiences nihilism or meaninglessness as any sort of threat at all. This means that for him, personally, the lack of explicit belief in this kind of God makes very little difference in regard to the meaningfulness of life.

The issue is whether those who do experience the abyss of meaninglessness as a real threat can find in process naturalism the reassurance that there is a ground of meaning. I do not myself find it there. I do find it in the panentheistic doctrine of God.

There are more specific effects of a panentheistic belief that may be easier to understand. One of these has to do with the habit of introspection. There are various reasons for being reflective about what is taking place within us, and not all of them are related to theism. Some of them are directed by therapeutic concerns; others, by scholarly interests.

But the biblical reason for examining one's inner life or heart is that God knows what occurs there and cares about it. What God knows and cares about has importance for us too.

In the biblical tradition and in the Christian history influenced by it, there is special and distinctive attention to motives. It is not enough that actions be overtly virtuous. It is equally important that they be performed out of righteous motives, especially love. To examine our own motives is not a pleasant experience, since at best we find them quite mixed. Indeed, a serious sense of sin and of our powerlessness to free ourselves from sin arises precisely when we examine ourselves in this way.

Taken by itself there can be little doubt that this sense of sin does more harm than good. But in the Christian tradition it is never taken by itself. It is always accompanied by the doctrine of God's love and forgiveness. The one who knows the heart—and knows its sinfulness—also understands it, accepts it, and forgives it. The more honestly we recognize our sinfulness, the more fully we accept God's forgiving love. This enables us to recognize the sinfulness in others without rejecting and condemning them.

Panentheism also makes a difference in the area of loneliness and companionship. Most of us at times feel that no human being really understands us or stands with us. This is a painful experience. Through the centuries this experience has led persons to turn to God. Given some doctrines of God, the results have only worsened the situation. But there has also been the sense that there is One who does understand, accept, and love even when the world seems to have turned completely against us. The doctrine of God we are considering here affirms this sense, undergirds and strengthens it. There are many who can testify that it *does* make a difference.

I have been reviewing quite central and common aspects of Christian teaching with which process theism fits well. I do not think process naturalism supports them in a comparable manner. This is in response to the challenge to show that belief in the panentheistic God makes a significant difference.

But the difference may not be one of superiority. There are those who feel that the strong sense of the meaningfulness and importance of human action that has been bound up with Christian teaching about God has done more harm than good, and certainly they are correct that it has done a great deal of harm. I believe that panentheism can lead to limiting the harm without losing the sense of importance, but that is disputable.

Similarly, the emphasis on sinfulness and divine forgiveness has had very mixed results. Many believe today that a different kind of spirituality would be far superior. Process thinkers generally support other approaches such as that of creation spirituality, and at this point the differences between process naturalists and process theists is minor. I personally believe that process theists can affirm creation spirituality and acknowledge the ease with which the focus on sinfulness is perverted into destructive channels without abandoning that spirituality altogether. But again, this is disputable.

Even the sense of divine companionship is ambiguous. It can encourage persons to give up the struggle to communicate with other human beings and to find a spurious surrogate in prayer. Such prayer, instead of being a source of fruitful action in the world, channels energies away from the needs of the world. It is just that kind of spirituality against which secularism properly revolted. I believe that panentheism can check this distortion without losing the positive value of the sense of divine companionship. But that, too, is disputable.

A very different way in which process theism can make a difference is in ethical theory. Ethicists often say that we should act as an omniscient and omnibenevolent being would have us act. This is a good principle. Indeed, it captures a very deep aspect of our ethical sensitivity. But disbelief that there is such a being weakens the argument that one should act as if there were. When one believes that this God of process theism exists, the argument and its potential for influencing decisions are strengthened.

Let us turn now to issues in public policy. One that has attracted considerable attention recently is biodiversity. Human beings are drastically reducing the number of species of living things on the planet. Most of these species are eliminated even before they have been identified by scientists, because of the rapid destruction of tropical rainforests. There is a spontaneous revulsion against this destruction on the part of many people.

It is interesting to see how this revulsion is expressed and justified in nontheistic circles. Usually it is argued in anthropocentric terms. We are told that some of these species might provide medicines that would be useful to our descendants. Others argue on ecological grounds, saying that the destruction of species weakens the biosphere as a whole.

Both arguments have value. But many of the species that are lost have no medicinal value, and the damage to the biosphere from the loss of most of these species is trivial. The revulsion is not in fact based on these practical considerations.

The revulsion occurs, I believe, because the variety is felt to have value in itself. A simplified world is an impoverished world. When the species that are destroyed are ones in which we humans have taken an interest, we know that our own experience is impoverished. But what about the disappearance of species of which we are unaware and which we would not find attractive if we were aware? Should we argue that our descendants would enjoy knowing about them? But is the difference between three hundred thousand and four hundred thousand species of beetles—to pose a question hypothetically—one that can really matter much in a human experience? I doubt it.

Really to understand the revulsion, we have to probe deeper. It stems, I think, from a sense that whether human beings can appreciate this difference or not, it makes a difference to reality as a whole. Reality as a whole is impoverished. But that implicitly means that reality as a whole is the sort of thing that can be impoverished—that is, that it has subjective qualities. Panentheism grounds and explains this judgment. For God the variety of creatures provides the contrasts that enrich the divine experience. I do not see that naturalism, even process naturalism, can provide a comparable explanation.

My second example comes from standard economic theory. This theory is based on naturalist assumptions of just the sort we are now considering. It assumes that there is no superhuman or inclusive experience.

The issue arises when economists want to compare gains or losses for some people with gains or losses for others. For example, many of us suppose that taking money from the very rich and giving it to the very poor causes much less loss to the rich than it causes gain to the poor. The loss to the rich family may mean that it must settle for a smaller yacht. The gain to the poor family may mean that each child receives sufficient food.

A good many economists would agree that in this case the gains of the poor outweigh the losses of the rich. But they cannot affirm this simply as economists. As economists they subscribe to the principle of "Pareto optimality." This principle is that since there is no one who can compare the feelings of loss and gain when these are distributed among different people, we can affirm a net gain only when some are benefited without any loss to others.

This principle has sweeping consequences. It means that when we turn to economists for guidance on public affairs, and when the economists function simply in that capacity, we are encouraged not to redistribute wealth but to increase the total amount. There is no sense of either minimal requirements or of sufficiency built into economic theory or the public policies to which it gives rise. An economic theory built on process theism would have very different results.

On these public issues I doubt that Mesle would disagree with the results for which I argue as a process theist. That is not my point at all. His challenge to me has been to say why process theism is important in distinction from process naturalism. My response in this case is that process naturalism does not provide a basis for clearly challenging the principle of Pareto optimality. Process theism does. It affirms that there is the One who includes, and can, therefore, compare, the feelings of loss or gain of diverse people. God experiences the benefits to the poor as greater than the loss to the rich, and we, believing in this God, can propose appropriate policies.

I have talked about two types of process theism and the differences they make. One is the focus on one kind of process in distinction from all others, namely, that process through which human good grows. The other is panentheism, the belief that all that happens in the world contributes to the inclusive life of the whole.

I affirm both. What enables me to do so is that the thought of Alfred North Whitehead embraces both in a coherent and convincing way. Whitehead shows in technical detail how God's immanence in the world functions to bring into being life and consciousness and love and to creatively transform all things. Whitehead's vision is completed in an understanding of how all creatures contribute to the divine life. Although there are process theists who follow Wieman in exploring only the former aspect, and others who follow Hartshorne in exploring chiefly the latter, many of us follow Whitehead in affirming both.

In these comments I have focused, as Mesle requested, on the difference theism makes. I hope that the reader will understand that, from my point of view, the practical difference is considerable at the level at which I have been writing. There is another practical difference that, I believe, is also worth mentioning. That is the difference it makes in the relation to communities of faith—in my case, to the Christian church.

Following Whitehead in affirming both God's creative and redemptive activity in the world and also God's loving reception of our lives into God's own, I find rich resources for the appropriation of my Christian heritage. As Mesle points out throughout this book, this appropriation involves also criticism and correction. But I experience such criticism and correction as continuous with the work of theologians in every generation. Process theists are proposing fresh ways of understanding the God to whom the Bible witnesses, ways that are often more faithful to the texts than was the classical theism with which we are often in disagreement. The relation of process naturalists to historic communities of faith is, it seems to me, a much more broken one.

I have tried to acknowledge along the way that I am arguing only for difference, not for superiority. Of course, I find the differences I have discussed to be advantages of process theism. Otherwise I would not be a process theist. But while acknowledging the differences one could argue quite otherwise. And certainly in our day, when the word *God* has become so confusing and negative for so many people, a strong case can be made for process naturalism.

Many of those who need a healing word most desperately cannot hear it when it comes in theistic language. Even those of us who are comfortable speaking of "God" must learn to speak also in other ways if we are to bring good news to those for whom "God" belongs to superstition, to condemnatory legalism, and to oppression. And for many of these, simply a change in language will not suffice. They sense the substitute names for the God they fear and hate, and they will have none of these. The only good news they can hear is good news that is fully naturalistic in the sense described by Mesle. To formulate process naturalism as he does can be truly redemptive for some.

There are others who would like to believe in the God described by process theists but who do not find the reasons given for such belief convincing. I do not believe that reasons for this belief, or for any other basic beliefs for that matter, are coercive. No one has come up with a completely consistent and adequate view of God and the world—or of anything else. What people find convincing and what arguments carry weight are affected by many aspects of a person's experience. For me, the empirical, existential, religious, and rational reasons for believing in God are cumulatively convincing. For others they are not. Sometimes this is because the way they think of God is, from my point of view, distorted. But sometimes it is not. Then I must simply respect them and rejoice if they can find in process naturalism a satisfying way to think and live.

Mesle has asked me to comment on other contributions that process thought can make. It is partly because of my interest in these that I ordinarily spend rather little time in the debate with process naturalists. I would prefer to draw their energies into some of the urgent tasks we share.

We share the basic model of a world composed of events that are complexly interrelated with one another. That is markedly different from the model that underlies political, economic, scientific, and ethical thinking generally. In all of these the mechanistic model still lingers on with its presentation of things as individual objects that can be examined in separation from one another. In my opinion, as long as most of our intellectual and scholarly activity is shaped by these outdated models, we will not be able to respond effectively to the complexly interrelated problems we face.

I have spent much of my energy in trying to bring the unsatisfactory assumptions underlying so many fields of thought to light and proposing better ones from process-relational thought. Even in this activity my theism makes some difference, especially because God is for me the ground of hope. But most of this work can be shared with process naturalists. And there is much work to be done! Several volumes in David Griffin's SUNY Press series on Constructive Postmodern Thought reflect the kind of collaboration that is urgently needed today. Also the irenic spirit in which Mesle approaches the differences about theism among process thinkers should help channel our energies into this kind of collaborative effort.

for further Reading

A good source of information about process theology is the Process and Faith Program of the Center for Process Studies, 1325 N. College Avenue, Claremont, CA 91711. Feel free to write with questions.

TWO EXCELLENT INTRODUCTIONS for persons wanting to take the next step after this book are:

John B. Cobb, Jr., and David R. Griffin, *Process Theology: An Introductory Exposition* (Westminster Press, 1976).

Marjorie Hewitt Suchocki, *God–Christ–Church: A Practical Approach to Process Theology* (Crossroad, 1989).

ADDITIONAL RESOURCES ON PROCESS THOUGHT:

John B. Cobb, Jr., *Becoming a Thinking Christian* (Abingdon Press, 1993).

John B. Cobb, Jr., *Can Christ Become Good News Again?* (Chalice Press, 1991).

John B. Cobb, Jr., *Praying for Jennifer: An Exploration of Intercessory Prayer in Story Form* (Upper Room, 1985).

David Griffin, *God, Power, and Evil: A Process Theodicy* (Westminster Press, 1976).

Charles Hartshorne, *Omnipotence and Other Theological Mistakes* (SUNY Press, 1984).

William Kaufman, *The Case for God* (Chalice Press, 1991).

David P. Polk, ed., *What's a Christian to Do?* (Chalice Press, 1991).

David P. Polk, ed., *Now What's a Christian to Do?* (Chalice Press, 1994).

Barry Whitney, *What Are They Saying About God and Evil?* (Paulist Press, 1989).

BASIC RESOURCES ON PROCESS NATURALISM:

Jerome A. Stone, *The Minimalist Vision of Transcendence: A Naturalist Philosophy of Religion* (SUNY Press, 1992).

Henry Nelson Wieman, *Man's Ultimate Commitment* (S.I.U. Press, 1974).

Henry Nelson Wieman, *The Source of Human Good* (S.I.U. Press, 1964).